The Dark Secret of Search Engines

Find out what search engines are hiding from you

FERNANDO UILHERME BARBOSA DE AZEVEDO

Table of Content

About the Author   3
Introduction   5
Chapter 1 - Understanding Search Engines   7
Chapter 2 - A Basic History of Search Engines   16
Chapter 3 - Search Engines in Numbers   32
Chapter 4 - A Peek into Search Engine Manipulation   37
Chapter 5 - Underhanded Tactics for On-Page SEO   47
Chapter 6 - Off-Page SEO and the Value of Backlinks   55
Chapter 7 - The Problem with Backlinks   63
Chapter 8 - Search Engines using Artificial Intelligence   72
Chapter 9 - The Dark World of Internet Marketing   82
Final Words   105

About the Author

Fernando Uilherme Barbosa de Azevedo is an electronic, electrical and industrial engineer graduated from Pontifícia Universidade Católica of Rio de Janeiro. He is MBA graduate from Fundação Getúlio Vargas. He has been a programming instructor at Pontifícia Universidade Católica of Rio de Janeiro for 7 years.

He published his first book "Macros for Excel hands on" by publisher Campus/Elsevier at age 27. The book is still sold in Brazil and Portugal.

His first startup business won a prize from the Brazilian Federal Institutional FINEP.

Coming to the United States in 2014, Fernando studied Web Development and Internet Technologies at University of California Santa Cruz - Silicon Valley Extension and also completed the "Innovation and Entrepreneurship Certification" from Stanford University.

Fernando has been featured many times in news media and TV. He was interviewed as a specialist on his field by Forbes, The Entrepreneur, el Nuevo Herald and many other major Brazilian media companies.

Today, Fernando runs 2 internet marketing companies in the United States and has clients in many countries. The companies offer services such as internet marketing, SEO,

Online Reputation Managements, pen testing, systems audit, e-commerce, apps and other internet related activities.

He is also a web development instructor for IronHack and weekly speaker at Radio Gazeta.

Fernando considers himself an ethical hacker and thinks that the internet should be a safer place. By advocating against all the unethical activities online that are still present today, he hopes that our leaders and law makers can become aware of these threats and help create laws for a safer world.

This book is dedicated to Fernando's sister Christiane Monnerat.

This book is a series of 5 books related to Internet Technologies and how the internet works. If you like this book, please check out other books from the same author.

Introduction

Search engines are the gateway to the internet. Google, Yahoo, Bing, DuckDuckGo and other help millions of people every minute.

These companies got so big, their indexes algorithms gained a lot of complexity, and have created millions of new jobs for SEO (Search Engine Optimization) agencies, Digital Marketing and E-commerce.

Search Engines are not fast and innovators like they used to be. They became the slow huge enterprises like following the path of IBM and Microsoft.

Search Engines want to be relevant so you can keep using them and they can keep money running ads. Is the most relevant article for the big majority really the most important article for you? Are you really interested in the tabloid link-bait over-the-top headlines that most people click? If it rotates around keeping the ads running, is everything we search trying to sell us something? Is everything we search trying to understand our values so they can better influence us into buying?

Meanwhile, outside of the Search Engines, SEO specialists work to manipulate their position on the Search Engines.

Also, digital marketers have carefully created each piece of content for you, sometimes showing evidence for arguments on both sides.

Privacy was not a concern till 2018 and companies were interested in increasing their sales by having our information and categorizing our social and economic aspects on search patterns and social medial information we give out.

Search engines are evolving to something bizarre. There are arguments for everything you search. There are ads for everything we search. SEO specialists manipulate Search Engines in ways search engines can't punish them. And even reputable websites are not free from biases.

Chapter 1 - Understanding Search Engines

To understand just how sophisticated a modern search engine really is, imagine that you need to do a book report on 644 million different books. They vary in size and in the number of pages they have. They also differ in the way they are formatted and in the language in which they're written. Some of them are for entertainment while others contain functional information. Each one has a unique topic and each author has a unique take. Also imagine that the contents of these books change from day to day. When a new topic arises, a page is added to that book. You will need to add that new page to your report. This is similar to what search engines are doing to all contents in the internet.

It would be impossible for one person to read books of that number. Before the digital age, for a person to find a book in a library, he first needs to go to the card catalogue area, look for the card of the book, take note of its location, and go to that portion of the library. Even if all the books are arranged and organized the right way, that person still needs at least 10 minutes to locate it and to bring it to the reading area.

A search engine helps us with this problem. It saves us thousands of hours when it comes to searching for information. It does this by indexing all the information into a database. To present users with information that's most relevant to their needs, the search engine must search far and wide to collect data from all searchable websites.

While it may seem like a simple thing to do, it isn't. A search engine that uses an indexing algorithm like Google uses computers to explore the internet. These computers are called crawlers bots, Googlebot, or simply just crawlers. They execute their programming by going to all the websites that they can explore, hopping from one website to another through links.

In the process, they collect relevant data about the website, its content, its important features, and many others. It then indexes these data to a database so that they can pull up specific webpages in the future when someone needs them.

In a nutshell, these crawlers read billions of webpages on a regular basis and keeps the index updated. As of the writing of this book, there are around 644 million active websites on the internet. Some of these websites have thousands of pages. Search engines organize all these in their indexes and serve the relevant content according to our search terms. With this in mind, we could break down the tasks of a search engine into three important steps:

Crawling

Crawling is the process of sending out bots to explore the internet and to collect data from each website they encounter. In our analogy earlier in the chapter, this process is like having thousands of robots read thousands of books at a time. It collects information from each page of every book.

Google, for example, encourages webmasters to optimize their websites based on Google's specification. They provide webmasters with a free tool called the Search Console. In the search console, they allow webmasters to submit a sitemap. The sitemap is like a blueprint of the website's structure. It indicates what webpages should be crawled by Google's robots. Ideally, all the pages in the sitemap should be interconnected by links.

By registering their website to the Search Console, webmasters are basically telling Google that they have a new online property and that they want their webpages to show in the Google search result pages. Google will eventually crawl the website and add its content to their index.

Even websites that are not submitted to Google via the Search Console are still crawled. Google reach these websites through other websites linking to them. When a Googlebot explores a webpage, one of its most important tasks is to check the links going out of that page. It then checks where those links are going. Through this method, Google finds new websites around the internet that it can add to its index.

When crawling websites, the Googlebot looks for key features in each webpage. It looks at the title of the page and sends back the keywords on them. It also collects metadata about the webpage. Metadata refers to information about the webpage that aren't visible to users but are still relevant to the Google indexing process. A webmaster, for example, could specify a meta-description for the webpage. Googlebot could take note of this information and use it when serving content.

In total, Google searches for hundreds of ranking factors found in the webpage and sends the information back to its servers for indexing.

Indexing

Indexing is the process of associating search signals to each webpage. Search signals are information that function like clues, telling the computer what kind of information is presented in a webpage. They come from the raw data collected by crawlers. While search engines use multiple factors to create these search signals, the two most important ones as of the writing of this book seem to be text content in the website and the links going into the webpage.

Although users now prefer a multimedia experience, search engines are still having trouble in accurately identifying the contents of image and video content. For both of these content types, search engines rely on the text content that comes with them.

Images, for example, have alt-attributes which serve as a text alternatives for indexing the image, serving as a text description of the file. When an image fails to load because of connection errors, the place for the image is replaced by the description in the alt-attribute. It is also used to help visually impaired users who are surfing the web through a text-to-speech function in their devices. When the text-to-speech software meets an image, it speaks the alt attribute.

Because search engines use the alt attribute as a ranking factor used for image search, most webmasters just stuff it with keywords that they want to rank for. This effect has made alt-attributes become less useful for their primary purposes. When a sight-impaired user meets an image in a webpage, he or she hears the ranking keywords targeted by the online marketer rather than a detailed description of the image. This is an example of how online marketers mess up user experience in their attempt to win the battle for search visibility.

Serving

When we use a search engine, we are only seeing the last part of their service. This is the part wherein they serve the content based on the query used by the searcher and the user-side information they collect.

In the case of Google, when a user enters a query, the search app on the device connects to Google's search server to access the index. It uses an algorithm to find the best webpages to serve to the user. The algorithm used is a highly guarded secret in Google Search. Most Google employees do not even know how the search algorithm works. Only a select few in the Google Search team have constant access to it. These people needed to sign non-disclosure agreements to protect Google's intellectual property.

On Information Gathering

The search algorithm used by Google sets it apart from the rest of the search engines in the market. In future chapters, we will discuss what we do know about the search algorithm. While it's a highly advanced form of technology, we will talk about how people are trying to manipulate it all the time. For now though, let's talk about the other types of information that search engines typically collect:

User-side Monitoring

<u>Location Tracking</u>

For search engines to actually succeed in providing us with the best content according to our search terms, they've decided that they also need information from their users. Just like all other websites in the internet, search engines collect a lot of information from their users. They use the IP address of the computer to get the user's general location. For mobile devices, the browser app may also ask for your location using GPS.

Search engine firms argue that your location helps their service. When you search for a pizza place, for example, they could use the location information collected from your device to provide you with a result close to you. They also use this feature to tailor fit the results based on demographics. A user from New Jersey searching the term "stock market", will get a different set of results compared to a user in the UK using the same query. The user from New Jersey may be provided with US-related pages, while the one from the UK will be served content related to the UK stock market.

<u>Search History</u>

Aside from collecting location information, search engines also create a search history for each device. If you use a query that you've used before, they will suggest it to you even though you haven't finished typing yet. These search queries can also be associated with an account.

If you have a Gmail account and you are logged in when you use the search engine, you may notice that Google will suggest queries that you've used in other devices. Let's say that you first used the query "Cheap laptops for sale" in your Android mobile phone with the Chrome browser logged in. When you go to your computer and use the chrome browser (logged-in to the same Gmail account), Google assumes that the mobile user and the desktop user is the same person because they're both using the same Gmail account. With this assumption, Google will make similar suggestions to you on that device. If you start typing the word "cheap" for example, Google may autosuggest "Cheap laptops for sale".

User Activity

Search engines also collect information about your activity around the internet. Google, for example, provides a lot of free services to webmasters, such as the data gathering services called Google Analytics.

This online service allows webmasters to track the number of users that enter their website. The service also allows them to find out where these users came from, where they are located around the globe, and what webpages they visited, among many other types of data. If the webmaster can see this, there's no doubt that Google also collects this data and uses it for their own purpose. We've seen time and time again that Google does not keep a service if it does not help their bottom line.

For webmasters to use this "free" service, they need to add Google's tracking script into their webpages. This tracking script allows Google to collect data about your usage even though you are technically already outside of Google's product. Aside from having Google analytics, the search engine giant also has an advertisement publishing arm called Google AdSense. Webmasters who participate in the Google AdSense program also add Google's scripts to their webpages to show Google Ads.

Google Ads not only collects information for webpages but also from apps and video content. This allows Google's data gathering mechanism to follow users even when they are no longer using Google search. Even if you are using a different browser, Google will still be able to collect data from you because of these free services they provide to their webmaster partners.

Search engines can follow you wherever you go on the internet. Have you ever seen an ad of a website appear after you've visited that website? This is an example of user tracking features in action. To serve ads, they use the data they've gathered about you based on your online behavior.

When asked about this, most search engine firms will say that their tracking tools are designed so that they can serve more relevant ads to the user. They will claim that it improves user experience. What they will not say is that the data they gather from these tracking tools are actually used to increase the likelihood that the user will click on ads. Together with your search data and the information they gather from your accounts, search engines know more about you than your own family members do.

Tracking Common User Behavior

Search engines have been collecting data ever since the industry started way back in the late 1990s. After almost two decades of collecting data, they have developed unique ways on how to use user data. One example is their collection of data regarding common user behavior. Long before we've heard about machine learning, search engines have been using it to hone the skills of ad serving services.

They use data collected from other people to help their machines make decisions in the future. Let's say that you're male and you have visited a lot of investing-related websites. There is a good chance that you've encountered a lot of cryptocurrency related ads in the past couple of years even though you've never visited a cryptocurrency website. Tracking tools collect data from internet users inside and outside of search services. These companies then use the data gathered to create an overall profile of the user. They match your profile with other profiles similar to yours. They could then adjust the ads that they show you based on what types have been successful in the past for your demographic.

By typing stuff in Google, for example, you are actually telling the search giant what your interests are and what are the events happening in your life. A woman searching for wedding planning tips is probably getting married or is planning a wedding for someone who is. This sends a signal to Google that the user may be interested in wedding-related ads. That woman should expect more ads about wedding planning services to show up while she surfs the net. Google will serve the types of ads that have proven to be successful to people with similar interests.

Again, search engine firms say that this method is primarily meant to help their own users have a better search experience. In reality though, there's profit involved. If they are accurate in matching ads with the needs of people, their advertisers are more likely to succeed. Successful advertisers are more likely to return to them to serve more ads. This in turn, leads to more profits for these search companies.

Ad Interaction

Lastly, search engines complete your personal profile by collecting information about your interactions with ads. If you've clicked on an ad in the past, you are more likely to be served with cost-per-click ads because they are profitable to run. On the other hand, if you have been profiled as a passive online user when it comes to ads, you are more likely to be served with cost-per-mille ads. With these ads, search engine firms are usually paid every 1,000 views.

Google is aware that the majority of internet users hate ads, especially if these ads do not match their interests. Because of this, they continuously look for new ways to serve ads that don't affect the browsing experience of online users. In the recent years, they have been experimenting on different types of ads that blend well with the surrounding content.

With this in mind, Google also gives each user the option to close an ad with the 'x' button in the corner of the ad. If a user presses this button, Google will ask that user for feedback on why he or she closed the ad. They would ask if the content is not relevant to the user or if it is obstructing the view of the content on the page. When a person constantly interacts with ads in this way, this sends a signal to Google that the ads are getting the attention of the user. That person is likely to be served with high cost-per-click ads that fit his or her interests and demographic.

The Cost of Automation

Ever since the beginning of the boom of the tech industry, search engines have been using machines to do most of the heavy lifting for them. Every task that could be replaced with an algorithm was replaced. They hired more engineers for quality assurance rather than getting more people to check the content that they serve and the ads that they run.

All the search engine and ads serving processes we've discussed so far are done by computers. The people they hire only make sure that the systems are working. They do not have any direct participation in the indexing and ranking of webpages. Everything depends on the accuracy of the algorithms commanding these systems to make the user experience positive and safe.

While this method of doing business has made search engine firms among the most profitable companies in the world, it also made them vulnerable to attacks. As we've seen in the previous US elections, big data can be used as a weapon against the democratic process. These events put into question the reliability of automated systems to keep our privacy safe. It also makes us wonder what information that we have in search networks can be used against us by international conglomerates or by state-level players.

Chapter 2 - A Basic History of Search Engines

The first search engine was not developed until 1993. Though search functions have existed in the past, they did not focus on providing a service to the non-geek users of the web. There were already some indexing attempts before 1993. However, indexing was still done in a very crude way. For one, there were no web robots in existence yet. The indexes at the time were done either manually by a person visiting each website or through a submission system wherein webmasters submitted their websites to be included in the index list.

The content in the early internet did not have a lot of value to the public. While news articles and blog posts are common today, at the time, the contents were mostly experimental. The community was mostly made up of tech professionals experimenting on what they could do with the network. It was unlike the internet that we have now. In fact, there were no browsers at the time that would remotely resemble the browsers that we use today. The rise of a publicly used web browser became the catalyst for the development of a public search engine and the other web services that we use today.

The first one to make a successful public debut was National Center for Supercomputing Application's (NCSA) Mosaic Web Browser. It offered features that were not present in its predecessors. For instance, it was the first web browser to allow users to bookmark a website so that they could easily come back to it in the future. Most text buttons were also replaced with easy-to-recognize icons. Before Mosaic, browser buttons were mostly labelled by text. These text labels took up a lot of space.

Mosaic became the blueprint that made future browsers possible. More importantly, it increased the number of internet users by introducing them to a tool that organized all the content in the web. While people finally had a tool to access the web in a user-friendly way, they still needed something that can search information from the web quickly. Several major breakthroughs in the same year made this possible.

Halfway through 1993, MIT student Matthew Gray developed the first Web Robot using the Perl Programming Language. He called the robot Wanderer. The robot collected information from all sites and pages, and put them in an index called Wandex. The primary purpose of Wanderer was to measure the size of the internet. Its true value, however, was that it served as the grandfather of the web robots we hear about today. Despite the existence of Wanderer and Wandex though, there wasn't a functioning search engine yet.

The first functioning search engines can be attributed to two services that came out in the later parts of 1993. The first one is AliWeb, which used an index but did not have crawlers. Instead, its information came from forms submitted by webmasters who wanted their websites to be included in the index.

The second one was called JumpStation. JumpStation was more advanced than AliWeb in that it implemented all functions that we still use in modern search engines. It was the first search engine to crawl and index webpages, allowing users to look up the contents of the index through searching. While it was in the right track, JumpStation had its limitations. For instance, its crawling and indexing functions only allowed it to check and gather information on the title and headings of the pages. This made it open to black hat manipulation of the search results.

The first search engine to offer full page indexing was WebCrawler. Unlike JumpStation, it allowed users to search the text contents of the page. Because of this feature, it became the most popular search engine in 1994.

Its dominance, however, would not last. In the succeeding years, other search engines were launched. All of them used web crawlers but they varied in the way they indexed the information they collected. One of the most popular among these early search engines was Yahoo. While it did use crawlers, its index was in the form of a web directory, similar to the directories we have now. Yahoo Search was severely limited though, because the contents it served to users only came from this directory.

Everything changed when Netscape, the most popular browser at the time, decided to find a search engine partner. The chosen search engine will be the default tools used in future Netscape browsers. While the original plan was to pick one, the popular browser ended up with a five-way tie between the search engines Magellan, Yahoo, Lycos, InfoSeek, and Excite. These five became the top search engines in this era with Yahoo becoming the most recognizable name.

While the search engine industry seemed mature, it was not yet the case. The search engines listed above all used different ways of organizing the information they crawled. The difference in indexing and assigning value to a page led to varying results in the search engine result pages.

The Rise of Google

It was two years later when Google was launched. The late 90s was still dominated by the big five selected by Netscape. Google, however, had something up its sleeve that other search engines did not. It all started with one paper written by its founders called *"The Anatomy of a Search Engine"*. In this paper, Google founders Sergey Brin and Larry Page developed an innovative metric for measuring a webpage's value. They referred to this metric as PageRank.

While PageRank mainly built on the architecture of its predecessors, it had one feature that changed the game. PageRank is an iterative algorithm that assigns a value on each page based on their desirability to the user. PageRank works on the principle that desirable webpages are likely to get more links from other desirable webpages. With this in mind, the algorithm assigns a metric on a page based on the number of incoming links. The value of each link, however, is not equal. It is based on the PageRank of the webpage where the link came from.

This new innovation gave Google a reputation among online users of being able to provide superior results compared to the other search engines. In short, for the first time in the history of the internet, people were able to find the content they want easily. It soon became the search engine of choice for most online users.

The rise of Google became the start of the fall of the other once-dominant search engines. In the coming years, Magellan stopped its operations, while Iktomi was acquired by Yahoo. Other search engines that went out of business were swallowed by other big companies. The domain names of Go.com and InfoSeek for instance, now redirect to Disney.

Other Notable Search Engines

It is important to note that the launch of new search engines did not stop just because Google dominated the market. In the same year that Google was launched, Microsoft tried its hand in search with the launch of MSN Search. Two years later, Google and Yahoo were dominating the market. MSN Search is still in business today but it was rebranded to Bing.

While Google dominates the English speaking market, other countries usually have different search engines that use their own language, such as in the case of China's Baidu. It was released in 2000 and is still being used today.

Google also has its limitations in the dark web. By the dark web, we are referring to websites that can only be accessed using special browsers like the Tor Browser. These types of browsers allow you to access websites with the .onion extension. While not all the contents in the dark web are illegal, the network tends to have the reputation of being a hotbed for illegal activities. The preferred search engine in this network is DuckDuckGo.

Development of the Search Community as a Business

The monetization of search engines began in its early days, specifically in the first half of the 1990s. It is important to understand that at this time, search engines were not considered as special websites by most people. Internet users didn't yet have the habit of opening Google or Bing when they used browsers. Some people used bookmarks, while others would assign their work websites as their home page. People just went to search engines when they had a need to look for something.

Because of this, early variations of search engines were not really specialized. The search bar for most search engines was included in a page with a lot of other features. Yahoo, for example, included all sorts of content in its search page such as news articles and links to games. They did this in an attempt to lure in advertisers. Today, search engines use keywords to target online advertising to the right people. In the past, it wasn't like that. Websites were paid simply for showing banner ads and text links for certain periods. Some websites were even riddled with pop ups in addition to the banner ads in their page.

This made the average webpage of the day, difficult to use. User experience for both the search engines and the websites were worsening. This peaked in the late 90s when the web industry began to boom. Nowadays, we remember this as the time of dot-com bubble that peaked in the year 2000. However, for those involved in the industry, the years prior to the bursting of the economic bubble was considered an exciting time.

At around this time, Google started the trend of removing all the clutter in the search homepage. Google went for the minimalist approach for web design which is common in today's internet. However, at the time, the common practice was to cram the webpage with as much text, images, and links as possible. For Google, banner advertising was not the way of the future. They had a better product for the consumer with the introduction of their PageRank algorithm. What they needed was a better product for the advertisers—an offering that's superior to the banner advertising techniques that were prevalent at the time.

Their solution was to sell spaces in the search engine results page (SERP) with the use of keywords to target the right people. Just like today, Google only used text ads in these pages. They showed these text ads in a similar way that they show the other organic results. However, in the past, the ads had a different background. Today, the background of the ads are the same but they are labelled with the word "Sponsored" to indicate that they are ads and they are not organic content.

The late 90s and the early 2000s was a time of rapid growth for the internet. It was the first time that the public had access to almost free ways of creating their own websites. In 1999, Blogger.com, a free blogging platform, was launched. It was later bought by Google. Similar blogging and website building platforms were launched in the early 2000s. The Content Management System Drupal, was launched in 2000 and WordPress was launched in 2003. Joomla and JQuery were launched a few years later in 2005 and 2006 respectively.

It was also in the late 90s that hosting services were becoming affordable enough for the everyday consumer. Likewise, personal computers were becoming less expensive. All these factors increased the number of products and service on the web and the number of daily users.

With the rise in the number of netizens, you could have guessed that the marketers were sure to follow. Each new website needed to compete in the ever expanding market of the internet. There weren't a lot of rules on how you could market your website back then. Because of the lack of a centralized governing body, people used all kinds of tactics to get noticed.

One of the primary targets of these tactics was the search engines, mainly because they were becoming the most used service on the web. Early online marketers had a lot to gain from gaming the search results. It was around this time in the early 2000s when the first SEO practitioners were professionalized.

The term SEO was first coined by an online marketer named John Audette. He used it in a meeting with colleagues who use the search engines as their primary way of driving traffic to their websites. The pioneers of online marketing usually had their own products to sell. Some of them sold books, while others sold the products they already sold outside of the internet. The number of internet marketers continued to grow. They met and exchanged notes through email, and an early form of online newsletters began to emerge.

It was through this online marketing community that the secrets of modern search engines were spread. Some people who had read the paper that Sergey Brin and Larry Page created, shared the ranking principles of the famous search engine. It became well known that Google used links and website content to rank webpages in their index.

It wasn't long before people began to exploit this principle. Instead of creating websites that focused on user experience, early marketers gamed the system by trying to rank on content that were not connected to their product or service. They wanted traffic and they were willing to play dirty to get them. This was a time of black hat internet marketing and it reflected in the quality of the websites.

Many consumer-created websites did not have their own monetization method. They did not have their own product or service to sell. To earn money, many of these websites used the ad publishing services that were already present at the time. It was around this time that Google created Google AdSense that allowed website owners to post ads to their own webpages.

These ads were also driven by the keywords that people used. If the user used the query "Bikes for sale" in the search engine, they are likely to see ads that are targeted to those keywords. Knowing this, online marketers made sure that their websites ranked high on the most profitable content in the market. Many online marketers, for example, would use keyword stuffing—a method where target keywords are inserted as many times as possible in online content. They used the keywords all over their page, even when they were no longer related to the content.

Aside from this, online marketers also gamed the PageRank algorithm's reliance on backlinks. People would buy hundreds of domain names, and then put up small websites riddled with links towards other websites. This black hat link-building technique allowed awful websites to rank high. With Google becoming the most used search engine in the post-2004 internet, it took the stand against the abuse of the search algorithm.

The answer came in 2012 with a few but impactful algorithm changes. The events are collectively called the Panda Algorithm Update. The name Panda comes from the last name of the developer who worked on the new algorithm, Navneet Panda.

At this time, many websites enjoying the top spot of Google Search were thin and of poor quality. Google wanted to change that. As a response, they made multiple tweaks in their ranking algorithm. While the exact changes in the algorithm have never been released, the effect of the change gives us a clue on what Google did. Generally, all websites with large amounts of advertising got penalized. These websites were once in the top spot of the first page. After the algorithm changes, they ended far from their original spot (6th-10th pages).

The websites that came out on top were those that had long-form content and matched the needs of the query. Early in the update, news websites got a huge boost, as well as social networking pages such us Tumblr and Twitter.

Aftermath of the Panda Update

The release of Panda though, was not necessarily a success for Google in the first day. Many of the affected website owners lost more than 90% of their traffic and their income. It is also believed that Google itself, experienced massive amounts of lost profits because of the update.

Right after Panda, many copycat websites also experienced some success. These types of websites are developed by scrapers. Scrapers are webmasters who just copy the content of other websites in the hopes that they will outrank the original content. Because of this and many other problems, Google continued to release updates. As the updates came, there was a significant decrease in the amount of content created by scrapers in the top ten search results.

At this point, the effects of the Panda Update have made a great impact on the search results landscape. Many websites that produced poor quality content and could not improve their websites closed up shop. Many content farms were closed all around the world.

Content farms are offshore companies that created text content for clients. The content they created underwent a process called "spinning". Spinning refers to a practice of duplicating the same text content by rephrasing the words and rearranging the order of sentences and paragraphs. Content farms have developed software tools to automate the spinning process. The content was then spread all over the internet for the purpose of linking back to the original website of client. This added more "link juice" to the webpage of the original page.

The Panda update made this artificial method of ranking obsolete. For many websites, however, the damage was irreparable. They had so many bad links that it was better for them to start a new website with fresh content than to correct their old black hat practices. Its effects were not just on individual pages either. If one of your webpages was deemed low quality and originally benefited from black hat techniques, the search ranking of your entire domain name was affected.

Many SEO professionals were shocked by the impact of the algorithm update. Those who persisted in the industry asked Google for guidance on how they could make a high-quality website. This led Google to release a blog post discussing what makes a high quality website:

Google's 23-point Guide on Creating a High Quality Website

1. Is the information on the webpage trustworthy?
2. Is the article written by an expert, an enthusiast, or a professional in the field?
3. Is there a copy of the article around the website that was just slightly reworded and rearranged?
4. Is the website trustworthy enough to receive credit card information?
5. Does the content contain obvious spelling, grammatical, stylistic, or factual errors?
6. Are the topics really needed by the website visitors or is the website just trying to game the search results?
7. Is the content of the website original?
8. Is the value of content in the page substantial compared to the other competing pages in the search results?
9. Has any quality control been done on the articles or the website?
10. Does the article discuss opposing sides rather than just one side of an argument (such as pros and cons of a product review)?

11. Is the website considered an authority on the topic by its users?

12. Is the content of the website part of a mass-produced network of websites to thin out the competition?

13. Was the article proofread or was it hastily created and published?

14. Would you trust the content of the website for health-related concerns?

15. Is the name of the website recognizable as an authority in the field?

16. Is the article complete or does it have a lot of information lacking?

17. Does the article contain information that is not obvious to the readers?

18. Is this the kind of webpage that you would share to people or bookmark for future use?

19. Does the page contain excessive amounts of ads?

20. Is the content in the page good enough to be printed in a newspaper, magazine, or encyclopedia?

21. Is the content of the page too short, riddled with the same keywords, and lacking in valuable information?

22. Was the article written with great attention to detail?

23. Would users complain about the content in the website?

Due to Google's blog post, many webmasters were able to adjust their websites to accommodate the changes required.

Here Comes the Hummingbird

After the Panda update, the next major algorithm change came in 2013. While the Panda Update was necessary to clean up the internet, the Hummingbird Update was needed to make sure that the search results accurately matched the needs of the user.

To achieve this, Google released an algorithm that focused more on the context of the entire query rather than the meaning of the individual words. At first, many people had fears that the Hummingbird Update would have the same effect as the Panda Update. Google quietly released the update two weeks before it was publicly announced. While Hummingbird did improve user experience in the search engine, it didn't have a great effect on the ranking of the websites in major keywords.

Current Search Trends

While Hummingbird and Panda were the most impactful algorithm updates, they weren't the only ones done by Google. In the years that followed, Google continued to release algorithm updates to respond to issues and black hat practices that are affecting user experience. They also adjusted rankings according to technological trends, such as the shift towards mobile browsing. Here are some of the most important Google algorithm updates throughout 2017 and early 2018:

Penalties against Intrusive Interstitial Elements

As Google is preparing for a mobile-dominated internet, they're beginning to attack website elements that may affect user experience on mobile. This includes features like pop-ups that do not fit the mobile screen or sticky banners that occupy a bigger part of the screen. Moving forward, all webmasters should consider the effectiveness of their interstitial elements before they implement them. It's also important to have user experience in mind (both in mobile and desktop) before adding new features to a website.

Shift towards Secure Browsing

In the past two years, the number of websites using HTTPS has been increasing. The HTTP letters in the beginning of a URL is the protocol used by the website to transfer data through the internet to the user's computer. HTTPS means Hyper Text Transfer Protocol Secure. The S in the end makes all the difference in keeping information secure. This change is done by contacting the domain name registrar of the website. However, changing from HTTP to HTTPS is equivalent to changing a webpage's URL.

Back in 2014, Google announced that it will give a slight ranking boost to webpages using the HTTPS protocol. In 2017, the number of HTTPS webpages in search results pages climbed to 50%. In the early parts of 2018, this increased to 75% tracked search terms in the US.

Webmasters should seriously consider upgrading their website to HTTPS as soon as possible. When doing so, it's important to focus first on webpages that require submissions. Hackers and data sniffers usually look for websites where the users need to pass information to the web server to continue. Information like passwords, usernames, email addresses, and financial details should be transferred securely to keep the private information of users from falling into the wrong hands.

Increased App Suggestions

In addition to penalizing websites with features that affect mobile experience, Google is also increasing app suggestions in the result pages. In the past, only webpages were suggested to both mobile and desktop users. Now, if a query matches some of the apps in Google Play, the search results page will also offer them as an alternative result. This will increase the competition for webpages that can be replaced by mobile apps.

If you have a web-based tool, for example, it may be worth the effort to create an app version of it. You will also need to optimize the Google Play page of the app to make sure that it appears in the search results.

Featured Snippets

Google is trying to keep their users' attention on the search engine longer by answering questions. The search engine does this with the use of featured snippets in the search results page. These snippets are boxes that offer the answer directly to the users. It is activated when the user enters a commonly asked query. Adding a "what is" before a word for example, will surely activate the dictionary snippet. This type of snippet looks like a box with the dictionary meaning of a word inside it. If applicable, the box may also include other dictionary features like synonyms, antonyms, and the origins of a word.

Asking direct questions also increases the chance that these snippets will be activated. If you ask a question like "When was Albert Einstein born?" you are likely to get a box that shows the exact date. As long as the answer is clear to Google, it will present you with a snippet for your question.

Snippets not only take away traffic for easy-to-answer queries, but they could also affect the effectiveness of the top spot in the search results. Some snippets have links that lead back to their sources. Because the snippets are always located at the topmost portion of the search results page, users will see them first. They effectively replace the top spot on Google.

In most cases, the snippet content comes from the website on the top spot of the search result. In rare instances though, some websites in the top spot of a query are not properly optimized to show rich snippets. If those in the number two or three spots are optimized, Google will show their content in the rich snippet box. This is why all SEO professionals are trying to master the use of rich snippets, aside from that fact that some of the most profitable queries activate them.

Transition to Mobile

In the past five years, there has been a continuous trend of people shifting to their mobile devices when accessing the internet. The scale has tipped so far on the side of mobile devices that Google has announced the implementation of a mobile-first algorithm change. This event is commonly known in the online marketing world as Mobile-First Indexing. As the name suggests, the algorithm change is all about how websites are indexed. In the past, crawler bots focused on the desktop version of a website first before looking at the mobile version. In this type of indexing, the desktop version is the first option to be offered when the search engine cannot detect the device being used for browsing.

With the Mobile-First Indexing Update, things have been reversed. Googlebot will look for the mobile version of your website first. It will also prioritize the mobile version when serving search results. This affects websites with no mobile versions. If a website faces stiff competition for its most profitable keywords and it does not have a mobile-friendly version, it's likely to get hit by this algorithm change.

Zero-result SERP

The zero-result SERP is still a rumor in the SEO world as of the writing of this book. The idea is that there will no longer be links to websites in the search results pages for some queries. Google of course, will be the one to decide whether this will be implemented. One example of a query where a zero-result SERP may be used is when a user enters a simple calculation, expecting to get a quick answer.

If the user for example, puts "3% of 2,000" in the search box, we could expect that Google will immediately understand what the user needs. If you search this before the implementation of zero-result SERPs, you will get a calculator with the answer (60). Google shows you a calculator assuming that you may have other computations in mind together with the one you just searched. Below the calculator though, you will see other results of links leading to websites.

With a zero-result SERP, you will no longer see the links below the calculator. Instead, Google may show you an option to show them. This will make searches with obvious answers load faster.

Many SEO professionals are wondering if some of their search traffic will be affected by this trend. The experts in the field believe that the queries with already effective rich snippets will be the first to go. However, we will need to wait and see how the zero-result SERPs will actually be implemented.

Chapter 3 - Search Engines in Numbers

Because many of the search engines in the early 90s went out of business, there's no way for us to accurately guess how the user base of the technology has grown in that period. What we do know is that today, the search engine with the biggest market share is Google.

Search Engine Market Share

In 2017, NetMarketShare.com recorded that Google held 81.72% of internet users, with Baidu in second place at 7.56%. Bing and Yahoo Search hold the 3rd and 4th spots with 5.56% and 3.94% respectively. The trend seems to continue in the first three months of 2018, with Google serving 79% of the market and Baidu serving 11%. While this may seem like a big jump, it's normal for internet use to be down in the early parts of the year. The search activity among English-speaking users should rise in the later parts of the year as we enter summer and the holidays.

Google has a clear dominance even when you filter the data only to show mobile users. In 2017, Google served more than 90% of the market, with Baidu only serving 5.44%. The continued success of Google will depend on how it expands in emerging markets. In 2017, only 46.8% of the world population accessed the internet. It has been growing steadily year after year and is expected to break the 50% mark by 2019. Statista.com predicts that by 2021, the number will rise to 53%.

Many of these new internet users will come from emerging markets. Governments now recognize the internet as a great tool for increasing economic growth. Countries that had poor internet connection in the past are looking for ways to fast track the infrastructure development for telecom companies, and this will bring in more internet users. Of course, not all of these new users will be English speakers. If Google is to remain dominant, it needs to be the first to reach the internet users of these countries. Baidu, while at second place, is not a real threat to Google's dominance in market share mainly because it caters to a specific demographic.

The Chinese-speaking market will always go to Baidu, while the English-speaking crowd is likely to use Google. The fact that China has a far bigger population than the US will allow Baidu to increase its market share, year by year as the number of internet users in China increase. However, this does not mean that it's taking away Google's market share. This merely means that China's internet penetration is improving.

It is also possible though, that Baidu will compete with Google in reaching out to emerging economies. China is aggressively building its diplomatic ties to become the world economic leader. While this push is mostly focused on the import and export of goods, the internet plays a big part in their plan. Their economic expansion plan is likely to succeed if their tech companies reach out beyond their own borders.

Baidu, being a state-owned entity, may face problems in entering new markets. Governments of other countries are wary of allowing state-owned companies to operate in their soil. This is especially true for industries like telecommunication and internet services. Allowing Baidu to become the primary search provider in your country basically means that you are allowing China to peak into the interests of your users. Google, on the other hand, while a US Company, is already an international conglomerate with ties to multiple governments.

When Google talks to the heads of state, they are not representing the US Government. Being listed in the US stock exchange, it is more accurate to say that they are representing their investors rather than the US agenda. These differences in the company structures may just be the factors that will make

Google succeed over its Chinese rival in the battle for emerging economies.

The Great Device Migration

In the past decade, users have been migrating from using desktops to different types of mobile devices. Mobile devices are generally cheaper than a desktop or a laptop. Their introduction to the market makes internet access cheaper for most people. Because they are portable, they also increase the internet access rate of a general user.

Using the internet on the go has become a reality. People are accessing the web in different ways in their downtime. The more time they spend online, the higher the chances of online marketers to get their attention.

While there are many other apps that are competing for the attention of online users, there is currently no alternative to using search engines. When there is a question in the users' minds, instinct leads them to use one. Their questions could range from topics about everyday problems to topics related to guides for purchasing decisions. The idea is that if I have this problem now, there's got to be someone in the past who also faced the same problem. Mobile phones have increased our reliance on the internet for solving these problems.

These are not just speculations though. They are supported by data. In 2015, Google announced that the number of mobile searches had overtaken that which were done in desktop. This was true in ten countries at the time, and it is even truer now, three years later. The general number of mobile internet users has also been increasing year on year. In 2009, the lack of internet hotspots, telco support, and the limitations in consumer technology prevented the mobile internet market from taking even just 1% of online users. At the time, 99.3% of users were using desktop computers. This was just two years after the launch of the iPhone and one year after the first Android phone was launched.

With these devices reaching more consumers in the following year, mobile internet access increased from 0.7% to 2.9%. In 2015, the number of online users increased to 35%. By 2017, the number of mobile internet users rose to 50.3%. Google has strong market position in the mobile area mostly because the Google Search app comes preinstalled in all Android phones. While Apple has a strong fan base, Android phones are more popular among budget users and those who want more customization options.

Search User Behavior

Search user behavior is one of the areas where most of the data collection happens. For example, did you know that most people use five words when searching? This is true for English speaking countries. When a person wants to seek new information online, they first try short keywords, often one to two words long. Searches of these lengths amount to 5% of all searches in the US. When people cannot find the information they want using one to two words, they often jump to using five to seven words. Five-word searches were the most prevalent, amounting to 63% of the total searches.

While this is all interesting, most of us aren't really interested in just any five-word query. Most online marketers are only interested in those words that translate to profits. In fact, in a 2017 survey of UK internet users, 54% of respondents said that they preferred to use Google search to research about a product they are interested in. Around 26% of users search ecommerce websites like Amazon to check online reviews. When used in this way, these ecommerce websites also serve as search engines.

Above, we talked about how people use mobile as their preferred search device. However, in the UK consumer research, only 11% of respondents say that most of their purchases happen in their mobile devices, and only 28% say that they do their shopping on a tablet. The most common behavior seems to be to use the mobile device for searching about the product, then using a desktop to make the purchase.

Of all the respondents who participated in this survey, 48% said that they used this method of researching and purchasing. Most people do not trust their mobile devices just yet to make purchases on them.

User Behavior based on SERP Position

Users also tend to discriminate results based on where they are located in the search results page. As expected, most people click on the top result. However, it's not as high as you would think. The top position only got a 31.5% click-through rate. This means that of all the people who saw the top position, only less than a third of them clicked on that result. This is the statistic for desktop devices. The number is even lower with mobile devices—a mere 24%.

The click-through rate though, predictably dips as a page moves down in the ranking. The biggest difference in ranking are between positions one through five. Results in second place only got clicked 12% of the total impressions. This dipped to 9% for third place and 6% for fourth place. Fifth place results only got clicked 4% of the total amount they were shown.

Using these metrics, a webmaster will be able to predict how much traffic his or her website can get depending on the traffic volume of the search query. For example, if the search query has a monthly search volume of 10,000, a webpage that ranks first on it will be able to gather around 3,100 visitors each month. This goes down to around 1,200 visitors if the same webpage moved to 2nd place. This is the importance of reaching the top spot of SERPs.

Chapter 4 - A Peek into Search Engine Manipulation

In this chapter, we will talk about how so-called search engine marketing professionals game the search engines and ruin the experience for everybody else. Let's begin by saying this:

Ranking in SERPs, especially those of Google, is big business. There are companies around the world whose sole business model revolves around getting the top search position. With millions to billions of dollars to be gained from winning in this game, we can understand why many are willing to invest heavily in ranking first in their target keywords. Because of the massive amounts of profit to be gained, a new industry called SEO was created back in the late 90s.

As we've discussed in earlier chapters, SEO stands for Search Engine Optimization and it is the process of using search factors to win the top spot in the SERP. In the following section, we will discuss the different techniques SEO professionals use to game the system:

SEO Auditing

Before SEO professionals start to make changes, they first need to do some research. First, they study the website and the company of their client who needs to do better in the search results. They try to find glaring SEO mistakes that may be causing the website to rank low. Most of them have a checklist of things to look for. Some of them developed these checklists from years of experience, while others just copy them from their mentors. They take note of the most common ranking factors like site speed, content length, keyword use, mobile responsiveness, and other factors that they may think are important.

Next, they study the competitor's website. They look at those companies that rank first in the keywords of their client. They use competition analysis tools like SEMRush and AHREFs to identify the factors where the competitors are superior to their client. Using these tools, they will be able to identify the keywords for which the competitors rank. They will also be able to identify the links going to the competitor's webpages. Lastly, the SEO professional tries to identify areas where their client's webpages can be improved for the sake of ranking in the most profitable keywords.

Keyword Research

After diagnosing the issues of the website, SEO professionals will look into the most profitable queries in their client's industry. They use tools like Google Keyword Planner and Moz Keyword Tool to identify the keywords used by those in the client's niche. They're not interested in all the keywords in the industry though. Instead, they only want the ones profitable to their client's business. This usually means targeting keywords that are related to selling the product or promoting the service of their client.

They target the easiest queries to rank for, especially those that have the most search volume. The shortest and most profitable keywords usually get a lot of competition. A lot of well-built and content-rich webpages with great user experience are trying to rank for the same content. A new website would have to battle for a long time to win in these competitive queries. Instead of working for these commonly used keywords, SEO professionals would sometimes use multiple types of longer keywords. This will give them an easier target to aim for. It will also give them results they can show to their clients.

In-page SEO

After identifying the target keywords, these SEO professionals now turn towards how they can improve the webpages that are already on their client's website. Instead of focusing on actual content and user experience, they usually put their attention on short-term fixes that would instantly improve the ranking of the website. This usually includes changing the theme of the website to make it faster or removing features from the website that may slow it down. They just want better positions in the SERPs. They do not necessarily care if the changes they make will lead to making a worthwhile website.

As a result of these quick-fix in-page SEO techniques, we, the users, tend to see the same features in all the websites we see. For instance, most webpages nowadays have a white background because it loads faster than colored ones. Also, all webpages tend to have outbound links these days, even when they're not relevant to the content. SEO professionals know that outbound links are important for ranking well.

These are only some examples of the cheap tricks that so-called SEO experts use. In the world of search engines, everything is guided by numbers. Because the ranking is controlled by an algorithm, the human factor is usually taken out of the picture. While Google's goal is generally to make a better user experience for their users, some of the ranking factors they use definitely do not support this. The preference for site speed is a good example.

Certain types of content and web tools require a bit of time to load. Some of them are digitally heavier but all that data is needed to deliver a tool that's more meaningful and useful to the users. However, these types of online tools and features are usually pushed to the back of the search results page because they don't load quickly. By putting site speed as one of the most important ranking factors, search engines are actually limiting the types of tools and features that a website can offer.

Off-page SEO

After doing all the quick fixes to create instant ranking results, these SEO professionals begin to focus on factors outside the website. There are many off-page search engine factors used by the algorithm. The most important one however, is the number and types of backlinks that a webpage has. Google, for example, likes to use links as proof that a webpage is a good source of information. They argue that great webpages tend to get a lot of inbound links from other reputable websites.

Unfortunately, this premise only works if people do not know that you are using links to rank webpages. If people don't know this, they will link naturally and great content will generally attract more great backlinks. However, because people know that links are valuable, they tend to change their behavior. By changing their linking behavior, webmasters have collectively changed the linking landscape on the web. Links are no longer naturally created. In fact, people tend to avoid using links when the only target page is in a competitor's website.

This topic, however, is so crooked that it deserves its own chapter. We will discuss it further later in the book.

Authority Marketing

Panda and the subsequent Google algorithm updates have improved the types of webpages that we see in the search results page. In the past, the top spots used to be dominated by spam websites that only offer information related to purchases. Some of these old websites only had a few pages, just enough to make a decent profit.

The algorithm updates changed all this. Nowadays, Google prefers content that discuss a specific set of topics. They want topics to be discussed in depth. These features create an illusion that the website is an authority on the topic. Through Google's point of view, if your content talks about one topic only and you have hundreds of thousands of words worth of discussions about these topics, then you are an authority worth sharing to the users.

The people who know about this unique ranking combination, however, also know how to game the system. Instead of working to provide users with useful information, they tend to put more information than necessary. Let's say that you searched for this query: "best gaming laptop under $1,000". With this, you expect content that talks about specs of laptops and in-depth articles about performance. Instead, you'd discover that the search results page is merely filled with underwhelming write-ups.

Many of them are just lists of products that have the highest review ratings on Amazon. The authors of these poorly written articles just add a paragraph or two under each product for SEO purposes. In these paragraphs, they only regurgitate the specs of the products—essentially copying the original product description. They also just repeat the pros and cons mentioned by users who reviewed the products on Amazon.

If Google's aim is to promote content that gives unique value to the users, then they are losing this battle. Those who dominate in the most profitable keywords are usually only focused on creating long-form content. They do not care to create new content or actually review products. Instead, their priority is to churn out articles as quickly as possible. After creating long-form content, they carry out backlink campaigns and automatically get the top positions in the process.

It's one area that Google still needs to fix because the content that they are presenting is neither unique nor authentic. The people who create these regurgitated content only want to generate profit from monetization processes, like affiliate marketing or Google AdSense.

Most people are wondering though, why Google hasn't fixed the issue yet with fake reviews. One possible reason is that they don't have better content to present in search results. But this is sort of a paradox. The reason why there aren't any worthwhile content in search terms like "best running shoes 2018" is because Google has been letting fake reviews win over authentic ones. They allow people who just know how to manipulate the system from taking the top spot without really considering that there are better content around the internet that just do not have links. Some bloggers, for example, write better content than affiliate marketing writers, but their articles are always buried at the back pages of the search results because they don't optimize them enough.

We could say that authority marketing is a sham because the people that Google and other search engines see as authorities are more marketers than actual experts in their fields.

Content Marketing

This brings us to the last step in the SEO professional's job. Content marketing is laborious and most SEO professionals think of it as a troublesome, time consuming task. However, for search terms that are harder to crack, this may be the only way.

The general idea is that websites and webpages with better results should rank higher. Even in this area though, Google is still failing. While the search results page has considerably improved since the Panda Updates, SEO practitioners have still found ways to cheat the system. The methods they use may not be as black hat as before, but they are still sketchy when you consider that Google's goal is to provide excellent content.

Google's algorithm still cannot distinguish excellent content from mediocre ones. Sometimes, the contents of websites have obvious mistakes that an average person can easily see. However, because algorithms do not know how to read nor do they actually know what is useful to the readers, Google still allows these poorly written content slip through the cracks.

Online marketers do this by dominating the same two factors we have discussed above: backlinks and content. In general, they just outwork other people who may be competing for the same keywords. It's not about creating the best content anymore. Instead, it's more about churning out numerous mediocre ones, which could be considered passable at best to the eyes of the user.

With these two factors in mind, SEO professionals hire writers from across the globe to create content for the client's website.

They may have reviews written for the actual products of the company or they could have their outsourced employees make random blog posts to make the website seem more natural. The general goal is to populate the website with content that revolve around a central topic. The more words they have on the website related to the topic, the higher they will rank on Google. They would then have these unimportant pages link towards their money pages.

In internet marketing, SEO professionals classify webpages into two: informational and money pages. While most of us only want information, they will try to lead us towards webpages that are designed to sell us products. A review post is an example of a money page. It's deep in the sales funnel and many people are looking for them. Even if you are just looking for regular website content, there is a chance that these gray hat marketers will constantly show you links in the content leading to their money pages.

To these people, it's all about herding people like sheep from the informational pages of the website towards the reviews, products, or services of the company. They are there to make businesses succeed on the internet, and many of them are indeed succeeding.

Through years of experimenting, many SEO practitioners have identified the top content that rank well in search engines. Many of them will not risk creating content that few people will search for. This is the reason why you see the same types of content all over the internet. It stifles the creativity of the overall market. However, it could be argued that search engine firms do not really care about this because even bad pages still help them with their bottom line.

Effects of Google's Inadequacies to the Online Marketing Landscape

Only People and Organizations with Money Win

Google has effectively created a landscape wherein only organizations and people with money can take the most profitable spots in the search results page. A new website can easily beat smaller websites that have been in the business for so long just by getting backlinks from big websites and reputable authors. When a site has links coming from websites like Time Magazine or Forbes, Google is more likely to trust it. The search giant does not know which links are actually paid and which ones just appear naturally.

Of course, having more money also translates to having more content. An owner of a new website can hire an excellent writer at a rate of $1 per 100 words. Writers at these low rates aren't amateurs either. Many of them have been writing even before the Panda Update hit the market. By paying for the services of a writer, these website owners will be able to outwork smaller websites. They may not necessarily have great content but because they get a boost from hired writers and paid high-quality backlinks, these websites will be able to outrank most of their competitors.

Creation of Fake Websites Designed only to churn out Links

While large-scale link farming has been eradicated, it does not mean that smaller-scale operations no longer exist. The spirit of link farming is alive and well. It just took on another form. Nowadays, link farms are called PBNs or Private Blog Networks. These networks are made up of websites of varying sizes. Some of them only have a few pages, while others contain hundreds of pages. All of them are filled with outsourced content (some acquired for as low as $1 to $1.50 per 1,000 words).

The websites in a PBN are designed to mimic a real web 2.0 website. They could be designed as a poorly written blog, while some could look like an abandoned website. The owners of these websites designed them for one purpose—creating link juice for their massively profitable websites.

Content Spamming still Prevails

In the past, content spamming means creating articles developed through spinning software. One article could be rewritten multiple times by a software and each one could be posted in a different website. The main articles tend to be used for a primary website while spun articles are used for link farms.

Nowadays, no content software on the market can cheat Google. Content spamming has evolved though. Because most SEO professionals know that Google prefers long-form articles, they tend to increase the number of words of their articles, sometimes unnecessarily. They fill their webpages with fluff content just to have a greater number of words (in comparison to their competitors). While it is not the ideal way to make content, it does work—and so, people keep doing it.

This method of creating content for ranking purposes is just another form of content spamming. Marketers knowingly manipulate ranking by adding unnecessary content to their webpages. While the content is vaguely related to the topic, in most cases, the users do not really need them.

Every Content on the Internet is designed to Sell Something

Because of the reliance of search engines on algorithms to do the work for them, they have created an internet landscape where every content is designed to sell something. Even instructional videos come with short adverts that are intrusive and most of the time, unrelated to the content of the video. The same goes with bloggers and content marketers who aim to rank high in SERPs. There is no accountability with these so-called experts who always plug 'related' products to unrelated content.

The Ones that aren't Selling Anything are Full of Ads

Even content aren't meant to sell something are often laced with ads. Most of these ads also come from search engine firms. News related to politics, sports, and entertainment for example, have few monetization options other than ads. Because of this, you will see webpages that rank high on the SERP having more than five ads published on them. Even these seemingly harmless content can now influence online purchases.

Chapter 5 - Underhanded Tactics for On-Page SEO

As mentioned in the previous chapter, many techniques used to manipulate search engine rankings still work today. The majority of these techniques are black hat in nature. By black hat, we mean that these techniques are in violation of content policies (especially those of Google). However, because so many people are doing them, it's impossible for search engine firms to keep track of offenders.

In this chapter, we will talk about the different black hat on-page SEO techniques used by online marketers to rank well on Google and other search platforms. A lot of webmasters use these techniques to compete because they work. This still happens today because search engine firms remain vague when explaining which techniques are allowed. Interestingly, many of those who use these techniques aren't actually aware that they are using methods that are against the rules. This is partly because their pages are doing so well in the SERPs. If it works, why change your methods?

Let's begin with the most common on-page black hat technique:

Keyword Stuffing

Using the right keywords in your website is important when trying to rank in the search engines. However, overdoing it could be considered keyword stuffing. In Google's point of view, for example, a webpage is using keyword stuffing when it contains exact keywords that do not serve a purpose in the content.

While using keywords excessively isn't really acceptable, people are still doing it regularly today. The reason why they get away with it is because they do it just enough not to get flagged. For instance, Yoast SEO, a popular WordPress SEO plugin, recommends a keyword density of 0.5% to 2.5%. This means that in a 2,000-word article, the keyword should make up 50 words in the entire page. This is too much and it does affect the reading experience of the user. However, because of their reliance on keywords, search engines still cannot let go of keyword volume as a ranking factor.

Hiring Ghostwriters

When analyzing the articles that rank first, SEO specialists can get an idea of what to write, how to organize it, the length it should have and all link-bait tabloid tricks that can be added.

Another factor that will make a page rank well is the frequency of publishing of posts in the website. If the website churns out content regularly, it will get more visits from crawlers. You will be able to observe this when you constantly check how a search engine renders a webpage in their search results page. Pages that come from authority websites like TheNewYorker or TheHuffingtonPost are usually crawled sooner than those posts coming from websites that only publish new content weekly.

This means that for a website to compete with the big content marketing companies in their niche, they need to churn out content regularly as well. This usually means creating content daily if a website is in a highly competitive niche. However, not all webmasters have the time to create news on a daily basis. Because of this, some try to hire ghostwriters to increase the number of new content that their websites publish.

While there is nothing wrong with hiring ghostwriters, the practice can sometimes border into the black hat realm when the webmasters hire based on the cost of the ghostwriter and not on skill or expertise in the subject.

A responsible webmaster will only hire writers who have experience in the niche they are writing about. A webmaster needing medical-related content, for example, may choose to hire people with medical knowhow such as nurses, aspiring doctors, or even paramedics. However, because of the lack of medical professionals who are also willing to work as writers, a webmaster often settles for the low-cost alternative. This usually means hiring someone from a developing country for a fraction of the cost of hiring writers in the US.

While there are some writers that do have the skills to create excellent content, the majority are often laced with grammar mistakes and awkward sentences. This happens because the writers are more focused on the number of words that they put into paper rather than the true quality of those words.

You may be asking why people are still hiring these types of writers when it could ruin their website. The answer is simple—the method still works. People still often get away with posting content with grammar lapses. While search engines can detect excessive grammar lapses, they do not directly punish content that have a lot of them. Instead, they let the user experience metrics (like time on page or bounce rate) decide whether the content is of poor quality or not.

This practice, however, only works among websites in low-competition niches. In high-competition niches like sports, entertainment, business and finance, or fashion, poorly written content will not work. The very people who rely on ghostwriters to improve search visibility are smart enough not to compete in these niches. Instead, they focus on topics and target query keywords that have low competition. As a result, netizens who use these keywords end up finding poor content.

Digital marketers can also order article with different conclusions and points of view. The compete over the attention for specific keywords and that can mean playing for both sides so they can get more traffic thus more revenue.

Using unrelated Web Tools to Increase User's Time on Page

It is also common for websites to use browser games and quizzes to increase the time spent by their users on their pages. In many cases, these tools are not related to the content they have, but are interesting enough to make new users click on them.

While such tools are not in direct violation of Google's policy, for example, webmasters use them to rank higher. These online tools increase the content word volume in their webpages. More importantly, the tools can keep the users engaged or more like, distracted from what they really need to be searching for. The time they spend on these tools improves the user experience metrics of the page and the website in general. Over time, this increased time on page also boosts ranking.

Stripping off Webpage Features

The opposite of the technique above is to strip the webpage of important features to make it load faster. While this has a positive effect on search ranking, sometimes it limits the potential of websites to innovate and to provide better services to their users. If a website's business model depends on competing in the search results page, this technique may be necessary. Bigger browser apps load slower, making them less likely to perform well in searches.

Content Scraping

Scraping is the practice of copying another website's content and using it as your own without adding any unique value to it. While it is obviously a black hat method and it's explicitly stated in Google's policy as one of the techniques to avoid, it is easy to pull off and to profit from.

Content marketers who profit from this kind of content thievery often try to find niches where there isn't a lot of competition but has huge potential in terms of traffic volume. Nowadays, almost all high-volume keywords and topics used on the internet have webpages dedicated to discussing them. A content scraper would focus on high volume keywords wherein the top pages in the search results have weak SEO profiles. If content scrapers, for example, see that the top content in a high volume keyword is less than 500 words long and has no backlinks leading to it, they may choose to compete against it. They do this even with topics that they are not familiar with.

Instead of researching about the topic and creating unique content, they often choose to go the easy route by scraping the top five to seven pages in their target keyword. They will then collect information from these webpages, identifying the positive ranking factors. They would usually check the keywords used in the title and also in the subheadings of the page.

After identifying these ranking features, they would then try to create their own content that has a more comprehensive coverage of the topic. They will try to combine the positive features of the websites that they copied content from. After that, they would beat all the other pages in the top five positions in the search results by going on a massive link-building campaign.

Content scrapers do not get flagged for plagiarism when they do not use the exact words of the original content. A user with mediocre rewriting skills but have excellent SEO skills can create content that can outperform the articles written by professionals.

Because of methods like these, creating unique content is no longer as profitable. There is no longer an incentive for creating original and well written content when someone could just copy it and get a higher ranking in the search engines.

Content Farming

When content scraping is done at an industrial level, you get content farming. This technique makes use of content scraping strategies and hiring cheap ghostwriters to create hundreds or even thousands of articles every month. These articles have multiple purposes. Some of them are used for creating PBNs. Google, for example, will not consider your websites as part of

PBNs if it contains well written articles and is constantly updated.

The websites that make up well created content farms look just like real authority websites, and some of them even serve well written content. They are also updated regularly, making them behave like real websites. Each content created in a content farming operation is usually highly optimized for search engine algorithms. For example, they are often made to be more than 300 words long. They're also devoid of grammar and spelling lapses through the use of grammar tools in basic word processor apps. Most importantly, they are all vaguely related to the target niche of the business owner.

If the articles created by content farms are of excellent quality, there would be no problem with this strategy. The only problem, however, is that many of them do not go through any real quality control or fact checking. Those related to finance, health, and law can give misleading and even flat out wrong information that may cause harm to the readers. You cannot really expect someone from a developing country, for example, to teach someone from the US about the best ways to resolve legal issues.

When a website is well developed and offer user experience, it won't get deindexed by search engines—even Google. Deindexing only really happens to those websites that have glaring SEO violations. Most people who maintain websites with content-farmed articles are in the borders of the black hat and the grey hat realms. The vast majority of them do not get deindexed—and might never be. Again, only those who had blatant violation will get the ax.

Content Spinning

A few content farmers still use content spinners today. Content spinners take original content and change some words to their synonyms. As you can imagine, some of these synonyms do not match the meaning of the original words they replaced. As a result, you get a lot of sentences that don't make any sense. Spun content can be easily detected by Googlebots, so the website owners mix them with articles written by low-cost freelance writers.

The websites where spun articles are hosted are not meant to be seen by real people because they are poorly written and most of them will result to high bounce rates. They are used for PBNs though, specifically to boost the word volume of the website.

Cloaking

Cloaking has also gained popularity after the Panda Updates because of their effectiveness in fooling the search engine algorithms. Cloaking involves the use of a software installed in the server that hosts the website. The purpose of the software is to redirect traffic. It first identifies the IP address of the user and matches it with the IP addresses of known search engine bots. Because many search engine bots never change IP addresses, they can be easily identified the software. Identifying Googlebot traffic is not a difficult feat for software developers. Website traffic tracking apps, for example, need to do this so that they can filter out bot traffic from real ones.

When the cloaking software gets a traffic hit from a known search engine bot, it automatically shows the bot visitor an alternative page. Sometimes the alternative page contains only a few changes from the original one. However, in most cases, the software shows a completely different page to the bot. The alternative page is supposed to be optimized for search engines. It's also supposed to hide any element in the page that may violate any of Google's policy.

This type of software is often used by people who are promoting content types that would make Google deindex them. A webpage for example, could contain content related to crimes, gambling, or even hacking instructions. Elements containing these types of content will be removed by the software when presenting the page to Googlebots. It then makes these prohibited content available to actual visitors.

Chapter 6 - Off-Page SEO and the Value of Backlinks

Off-page SEO covers everything done outside a website that has an effect on rank. In most cases, this is about authority sites promoting other websites through mentions or links in their content. Although search engines have reduced the importance of inbound links in achieving the top spot in SERPs, having enough links (from the right sources) is still crucial. Without them, a page will have limited search visibility even if it provides accurate, up-to-date information.

Inbound links or backlinks can be categorized into three types: natural, manually built, and self-created. Natural links are arguably the best of the three since they do not require any action from the site owner. These are given freely, usually as part of reviews, recommendations, and top lists. Manually built links, on the other hand, are acquired by asking people (such as customers and influencers) to link to a website. Lastly, self-created links are those usually added to directories and comments by the ones running or managing the site. Although this type used to be popular several years ago, it's currently considered risky since search engines tend to flag it as black hat.

More Complex than it Seems

Aside from choosing among these types of backlinks, SEO professionals and site owners alike consider signals that affect how beneficial a backlink can be. Among these signals is authority. Simply put, getting inbound links from a page or domain that does well in the SERPs is much better than receiving backlinks from a site that barely has search visibility. Popularity and trustworthiness are similar signals in the sense that they are mostly associated with established websites.

Freshness also plays a role in determining the effectiveness of a backlink. The newer the linking page is, the more capable it is of improving the linked page's search visibility. As you would expect, just being new won't do, especially since authority, popularity, and trustworthiness are all key signals. It is likewise important that the topic between the two linked pages are actually related. During the early years of SEO, people did not care about matching topics or content when building links. This resulted to poor quality entries in SERPs that severely affected the public's search experience.

Search engines have also started to pay attention to anchor texts. Linking to websites with generic anchor texts (such as *click here*) will no longer yield positive results. SEO professionals and site owners now have to avoid putting too much keywords in the anchor text. Moreover, topic relevance, a signal that we have previously discussed, plays a role in determining the appropriateness of an anchor text. The source page's topic should match the anchor text's content.

With these signals, it's clear that search engines have really been improving as of late. They have identified issues that led to poor results in the past. Linking unrelated content or domains, for example, will no longer have positive effects on search visibility. It is even more likely that such a tactic would lead to worse placement in SERPs.

Click-Through, Time on Site, and Bounce Rate

Regardless of how important these backlinks may seem, they are only one part of the off-page SEO equation. In order for them to be of any real worth, they need to bring in people. This is where click-through rate (CTR) usually gets discussed. It is, after all, the ratio of people who end up clicking on a link, to those who only viewed the link. The CTR is generally viewed by marketers as a metric of success, despite its obvious limitations.

Knowing whether a visitor actually liked the page's content, for example, would be impossible by just checking the CTR. As you would have guessed though, this metric remains popular due to its sheer simplicity, particularly in the ease at which it can be acquired and analyzed. SEO professionals and site owners who need more detail and better insights often pay attention to two additional factors: time on site and bounce rate.

Time on site (also referred to as dwell time, average time, or duration) is literally the amount of time a visitor spends on a given page. Of course, this is not something analyzed on a per-visitor basis. Averages are taken and afterwards interpreted. There is no generally accepted minimum for a page's time on site to be considered good. A good time on site depends on the website's niche and complexity, among other things.

For example, pages that cater to the academic crowd normally have higher time on site averages compared to pages from other niches. This can be attributed to the fact that scholarly articles and resources require careful reading. The need to check any linked references for credibility may further add to the time spent on each page. Pages that mainly show funny images or clips, on the other hand, won't require as much time to appreciate.

Even though there is no generally established value for a good time on site, it is considered bad for any page to only manage to keep visitors for less than half a minute. While Google and other search engines do not explicitly list time on site as a factor in determining search visibility, it is only appropriate to believe that it is. After all, search engines are starting to shift towards a user-centric approach in determining search results and rankings.

As a metric, bounce rate is a lot more straightforward compared to time on site. Bounce rate is the percentage of visitors who end up leaving a site after viewing a single page. Having a high bounce rate obviously has a negative effect on rank, despite the lack of confirmation from Google and other search engines that it is indeed a factor. Keep in mind that even if a user leaves the SERP, it's still possible for search engines to keep track of things. Knowing whether the user simply returned to the SERP should be easy.

SEO professionals and site owners usually aim for bounce rates of around 40 to 55 percent. Of course, there are established websites that fall within the 25 to 30 percent mark, meaning they have superb bounce rates. Websites that have bounce rates of 70 percent and above are considered poor. These are often the ones that have a hard time attaining good search visibility.

With bounce rate being a hidden metric in determining search rank, it once again becomes clear that search engines are changing for the better. They are trying to close loopholes that have been abused for so long. Domains that only drive clicks but fail to manage to keep visitors engaged (whether due to subpar or entirely unrelated content) would no longer enjoy excellent placement in the SERPs.

Gaming the System with Specialized Tools

Unfortunately, even with these improvements, people are finding ways to maintain an unfair advantage. Link-building software are still quite popular despite search engines becoming stricter. While there is always the possibility of being flagged and penalized from using these programs (despite the fact that many of them have "safety" features in place), many seem to believe that the gains are worth the risk. Here are a few examples of these link-building software:

Money Robot

SoftTech, the company that developed Money Robot, takes pride in the fact that they allow people to tap into the power of web 2.0 without exerting much effort. Web 2.0 websites are generally preferred by search engines and thus, offer more valuable links than Web 1.0 websites. Just to be clear, Web 2.0 websites are those that mostly feature user-generated content and can be navigated easily regardless of skill and device.

SoftTech claims that their link-building software takes full advantage of artificial intelligence. This supposedly makes Money Robot capable of tricking search engines into thinking that actual people are doing every action in the link-building process. Is this true? Given that those who rely on this application still finds it necessary to hide their IPs, clearly the AI isn't as good as they would like it to be. In the case of Google, when an IP gets flagged for automated queries and other similar things, it is temporarily prevented from doing using search.

RankerX

Launched in 2016, RankerX guarantees first-page ranking. That is definitely a tempting offer for anyone willing to take shortcuts in SEO. It works in a way similar to Money Robot, although it claims to be highly effective for marketing video channels and content—particularly those that present quick fixes and in-demand guides. It also comes with niche-targeting and one-click automation features to further simplify the link-building process.

If you look at RankerX's website though, you will notice that it is somewhat shady. Only the *Buy Now* page works (the other pages seem to be blank) and there are obvious proofreading errors throughout. Searching for reviews about the link-building software is also problematic as you will mostly end up finding ones loaded with praises. Nevertheless, even if RankerX does work, there's no guarantee that any rank boost it gives will remain in the long term.

Once search engines identify the domains being used by RankerX, any site that depends on them will expectedly experience a drop in rank. At this point it becomes clear why the software only comes with a 30-day money back guarantee despite costing roughly a thousand dollars.

SEnuke TNG

SEnuke is priced much lower compared to RankerX despite promising the same things, including first-page ranking. It also seems to be more aggressive and comes with added features like Google Places integration, article spinning, and macro recording. The problem with this encompassing approach is that the software puts domains at risk of being flagged for all sorts of offenses, many of which are easily detected.

The article spinning feature, for example, does not do a good job of making unique copies of articles. It simply creates poorly reworded content and publishes them on dozens of low quality websites. While it is possible to get a temporary boost from this approach, it is obvious that the recipient of all those backlinks will eventually get flagged for poor quality links and content spamming.

There is also the option to do link building without having to write or spin articles. The software does this either by getting existing articles online and spinning them, or by making use of scraped content. Both these approaches have one serious downside—getting penalized for plagiarism is practically guaranteed. This, combined with the low quality link and content spam, is why many who have invested in SEnuke end up dropping it after a month or two. And yes, most of those who have used SEnuke have had their websites completely deindexed.

SEO Autopilot

Quite similar to Money Robot with its focus on Web 2.0, SEO Autopilot is a safer choice compared to most other entries on this list. Regardless of that, however, the main risks stay the same. Automating the backlink building process, even if high quality assets and domains are involved, could end up putting a website in the watchlists of search engines. Again, no matter how effective these automated solutions may seem at the start, their methods will eventually be identified—and anyone who benefited would get penalized.

xRumer

Popular roughly a decade ago, xRumer used to be among the top tools for those wanting to spam forums with links. When search engines began to take action against this approach though, people shifted to a less risky strategy. They instead used the software to automatically post links on forum profiles. Of course, most forum administrators considered this unacceptable and started to work against spammers that relied on xRumer.

Although generally known as a forum-posting tool, the current version of xRumer comes with a variety of features that allow it to compete with other link-building programs. It even has plugins for social media (though mostly those popular in Russia) and comes with captcha bypass functions. Now that it has all these "competitive" features, however, using it has become riskier as well. It became comparable with its competitors, even in terms of the downsides involved.

ScrapeBox

ScrapeBox is another program that automates comment posting, albeit marketed towards SEO professionals and site owners who wish to focus on blogs. Similar to the other tools we have listed so far, ScrapeBox has a number of built-in functions like keyword harvesting. It even has its own proxies that help black hats in keeping their IPs safe from temporary bans. As to be expected though, there are risks involved in using any of ScrapeBox's features even with a masked IP.

No Hands SEO

Touted as a 24/7 backlinking solution, No Hands SEO peaked in popularity a couple of years ago. Similar to other link-building tools, however, its users started to drop in 2016. SEO professionals and site owners started to transition to a more careful approach when it comes to improving search visibility, especially since Google and other search engines have begun to penalize poor quality, mass produced links.

Even though Pure Business Logic, the company behind No Hands SEO, promises continuous updates to the software, it's unlikely that applications like it would ever become as "useful" as they once were. Still, that does not mean that loopholes and underhanded techniques involving backlinks have ceased to exist. As you will discover in the next chapter, there are new ways in which black hats take advantage of backlinks.

SEO Agencies

The best SEO Agencies have their custom software, sometimes using one or more of the softwares above. They can create a large network of domains that receives fresh news automatically. They can even be specialized in some niches like Workers' Compensation Lawyers and dominate all search results pages on keywords related to their niche.

Chapter 7 - The Problem with Backlinks

As you have learned in the previous chapter, backlinks refer to hyperlinks from other websites that are going into a certain webpage. It's still one of the most important ranking factors in the SEO industry. The idea is that if more people are linking towards a website, its content is generally deemed valuable. It's so valuable that other webmasters and site owners are recommending the website to their own readers. Search engines see this as a good sign of the website's value.

In the past, it was all about the number of links you had going to your website. The more you had, the higher you rank. Google, however, found that many website owners were gaming the system. They would pay link farms, which are black hat businesses that made worthless websites just meant to create links and sold to website owners. These link farms would offer thousands of links for as low as $20.

In response to the growth of link farms, Google adjusted its reliance on backlinks as a ranking factor. The number of links, though still important, is no longer as powerful as it used to be. Five years after the Penguin Update, many SEO professionals are still in the dark on the true value of backlinks.

Links: Quality over Quantity

In the past five years, Google has been improving its technology in detecting the value of each link. The idea is to make links from active, longer running, and well developed websites more valuable than those that come from poorly built ones. This and the increase in value of other ranking factors (like quality of content) are responsible for the improvement in Google's search results.

While this improvement is welcome, Google's reliance on backlinks as a ranking factor is definitely not foolproof. Techniques that artificially increase the amount of links that a website has is generally referred to as link-building schemes. If your website is found guilty of carrying out such a scheme, it will get penalized by having its pages pushed to the back of the search results. A webpage that was in the first place for example, is pushed back to the 50th position in the search results page. If a website is guilty of being a link farm or engaging in any massive link-building schemes, it will even be deindexed by Google.

Deindexing of Worthless Websites and Violators

Being deindexed is an online marketer's worst nightmare. When a website is deindexed, it is no longer ranked in certain query terms. For these particular terms, your pages are no longer going to show up. It's like your webpage has been removed from the internet. In the Google Search Console, you will see your stats go down to zero instantly at this point. You will also get massive decreases in traffic.

Google does this for English websites that do not fall within their standards and are not really providing anything of value. Having a bad website alone is not against the policies though. It will only be deindexed when the website begins sending out massive amounts of do-follow links to other websites. If this is the case, Google may suspect that the website is being used as a part of a PBN.

A Game of Cat and Mouse

Many SEO professionals argue that the way Google and other search engine companies use backlinks is rather problematic. The more a page is linked to, the higher it ranks. However, if the link-building process is happening too fast, search engines immediately assume that something fishy is going on and may proceed to penalize the content. Also, linking to a page using an industry keyword in the anchor text improves that page's rank for related keywords. However, if one keyword is used too often, it leads to a page getting penalized.

With this system, established websites such as those of news outlets and media companies tend to collect the most backlinks. However, this does not always mean that they have the best content. In some cases, these websites are not updated for years but still remain in the top spot of the search results.

Backlink strategies have also improved through the years. Despite this, Google still keeps an eye on all of them to catch violators. In Google's eyes, any tactic used to artificially boost search engine rankings is a violation of the rules. This includes techniques that were regarded as legitimate in the past. Guest posting is one of the best examples for this. Back then, people thought of guest posting as a white hat technique for generating valuable links. With guest posting becoming popular among online marketers, links from legitimate websites (like those of daily publications) became coveted. Some websites even relied on guest posts as a way to generate new content at no cost.

Eventually, Google decided that the technique has become overused and many guest posts were made only for ranking purposes and because of this, many of them were poorly written. Now, guest posting is listed in Google's examples of link-building schemes. This means that Google only wants website owners to generate backlinks through natural means. In most cases, you can only get links this way through sheer luck.

These examples and many others like it tend to make the link-building process confusing. In fact, making the process confusing may just be Google's goal. With most people in the dark with the importance of backlinks and their effectiveness in achieving better search visibility, most webmasters just forego with their backlink building efforts. Likewise, those just starting their own websites choose to simply focus on content development.

A website that generates backlinks too fast in a highly profitable keyword will catch Google's attention. Sometimes, they do let one of their employees manually check the link profile of a website. If they find that the links are from fake sources, the website may end up losing its precious ranking. Instead of doing aggressive link-building campaigns, Google wants websites to focus more on content—well, at least that seems to be the plan.

Private Blogging Networks

While Google has gone to great lengths to make its search results page useful and clean, they are still vulnerable to manipulation. Many websites still get away with manipulating the rankings through clever ways of creating great link profiles.

They do this through the use of PBNs. A PBN is used to indirectly boost the link profile of a website. The developers of these networks know that directly spamming links to a website will not work. Google will know whether the links are coming from fake websites and will just penalize both the recipients and the members of link network. They have successfully eliminated link farming through this method.

To circumvent Google's methods against link farming, PBNs were made. As we've briefly discussed before, a PBN is composed of websites that are filled with cheaply purchased content. To keep the cost low, they are usually hosted in free services like Blogger, Weebly, or WordPress.com. Some PBNs are also hosted on cloud platforms and other hosting services specifically used for PBNs. Companies offering PBN hosting services claim that they can provide each website with a unique IP address. This prevents the websites from looking like they're from one source server.

The websites in these PBNs are not totally worthless. They may serve ads to make money for the PBN owners. Most of them, however, are only developed until they seem legit to the search engines. For some websites, this may mean creating around 10 posts. In some cases, the PBN owner fills the site with as much as 30 posts with a minimum of 300 words in each of them. The members of the PBN are then used to link towards a secondary website. This will boost the link profile of the secondary website. The technique works best if the secondary website is a legitimate news or magazine website. Websites like Forbes or The Huffington post, for example, accept contributors.

To illustrate, let's say that you have a website and you want one or your webpages to rank well in search engines. Together with your primary content, you also created a long-form article that can be used for guest posting. You then write to popular news and magazine websites, offering your services as a part-time contributor. If they accept contributors, they will likely have people contact you to send your draft. You then send your draft to them for checking.

If they like it and there aren't a lot of articles in line for publishing, they may accept your draft with editing suggestions. If the deal pushes through, you may get your content published and acquire a link going to one of your webpages. Also, instead of directing your PBN links towards your own website, you point it to the guest post for targeted keywords. This will boost the link profile of the secondary page, and in turn increase its value.

Lastly, the secondary website is made to link back straight to the main website. In theory, the link juice of the secondary website from the links of the PBN will pass on to the main website. In most cases, when a query is not profitable enough to invite white hat webmasters, the main websites of a PBN tend to get the better rank. They usually outrank smaller blogs and small business websites whose contents offer better user experience.

The Danger of PBNs

While there is nothing wrong with this model if the content is harmless, PBN websites usually target those queries that are highly profitable but have fewer competing websites. In the process, they usually create contents like product reviews and service advice that affect the reader's purchasing decisions. These types of content are dangerous when they promote products or services with profit as their top priority.

A website owner, for example, may only promote products that have the highest profit margin for them. Even though they know that there are better products on the market, they may choose to avoid endorsing them because they don't bring in good enough profits. When profits are the basis for providing purchasing advice, you could say that the website owners do not necessarily have the audience's best interest in mind. They may end up giving horrible advice—but because the users trust them, they're essentially influencing people to make bad decisions.

Mastermind Networks

A mastermind network works like a PBN but isn't handled by a single individual. In this case, a group agrees to exchange links to boost search rankings. A mastermind network usually forms between people who are in the same niche. Those involved are usually marketers who are not competing with each other but have websites in the same industry. A movie blogger, for example, would partner with someone who owns an ecommerce website that sells movies.

It usually starts out with just a pair of website owners but eventually spreads out and gets more people involved. The idea is to mention the other person in one's blog post or article and in the process, add a backlink to their website. This passes off link juice towards the recipient. In a future article, the other person will also do the same, thereby completing the exchange.

This kind of exchange often happens naturally when professionals meet one another. However, the difference between building backlinks naturally and running a mastermind network is that the latter is deliberately done to increase the link profile of each website in the network. The value of a person's membership in the mastermind network depends on how many domain names he could add to the link profile of the other members.

Unlike PBNs, mastermind networks have a higher chance of success in getting the member websites to rank high because each member is a legitimate website. In fact, because the links in networks like these are built slowly, many people who use these techniques experience success in long periods.

Backlink Software

In the past, backlink-building software was used for automating the backlink building process in a backlink network. You may have already guessed that this process no longer works.

As Google adjusted its policies in dealing with backlink spamming, backlink software services have developed to help webmasters locate links from profitable websites. The goal of these link-building software services is to find dead links. Dead links are hyperlinks that lead to deleted pages. This happens when the page that is linked to is deleted or if the domain name has not been renewed by the webmaster. There are many dead link checkers on the market. Some are free while others come with SEO tool bundles.

Some backlink software solutions go beyond just looking for dead links. Ahrefs.com and SEMrush.com offer comprehensive backlink campaign planning and analysis tools. Both offer tools for checking the backlink profile of a website's competitors. Services like Linkio.com push things even further by comparing specific link profiles to those that are in the top spots in the search results page. You will know where the most effective links come from and what anchor texts are being used.

Experienced web administrations avoid any service that promises to automate the link-building process without requiring any participation. Most of these services merely rely on poorly developed PBNs. We will discuss more on this in future chapters.

The Backlink Paradox

So far in this chapter, we've discussed how Google and other search engine companies deindexed webpages with contents and SEO practices that violate their policies. Simply put, deindexing is meant to keep the internet a clean and safe place. Deindexing, however, is sometimes used by black hats to remove their competition from the search results, this technique is called Negative SEO.

Just like with many other operations carried out by search engines, the deindexing process happens automatically. Once a webpage raises enough red flags, it's automatically deindexed. Because of this, a third party can orchestrate a scheme to make it seem like a website is using black hat techniques, especially in relation to the use of backlinks—and this is what we call the Backlink Paradox.

One way to do this is to use a PBN that has been flagged by Google. When Google detects a PBN, it deindexes all the websites included in it and penalizes all the webpages that benefit from it. Not only is the link juice removed, the webpages that make use of the PBN are also punished by being pushed to the back of the search results page. Knowing this, it should not surprise you that there are companies that offer PBN attacks to website owners in competitive niches.

Again, they use PBNs that are already flagged by Google. These PBNs were not necessarily meant to be attack networks. In the past, they were used as regular linking networks. Over the years, however, Google caught wind of the network and decided to deindex all the websites involved in it. The people who built these PBNs know when their network has been compromised because all the websites that feed off from their link juice has their ranking affected.

Another way it to use spammy backlinks software to create millions of low quality backlinks like non-sense blog comments per day. Google can flag this website was doing black hat and punish their backlinks, even if the action was solely orchestrated by the competitor.

Big authority websites are immune to this because they already have a great domain profile in Google's index. The possible victims are those smaller websites that just ranked well in search because of their excellent content. When a PBN or spammy links known to Google is used to link to the target website, it may be affected by the negative links. Website owners may disavow these links but this could be difficult if they do not know which ones are causing the problem.

In the chance that deindexing is prevented, this may still cause the target website to be kicked off the first page of the search results. It may take the site weeks or even months to get back to the first page. In this time, that website would have lost a considerable amount of income from the lost traffic.

Chapter 8 - Search Engines using Artificial Intelligence

Search engines started out as simple algorithms matching keywords with the content in webpages. The indexing method has evolved since then. A decade after Google first set up shop, search engines are now using artificial intelligence or AI to serve better results to their users.

While AI may seem like futuristic concept, it's beginning to be used extensively in many industries. It is no surprise that the biggest tech company in the world is starting to use it as well. To make the concept of artificial intelligence more believable, Google doesn't necessarily call it AI. While their technology technically falls within the scope of artificial intelligence, they prefer to use specific terms that relate to the services that can be offered through it. For instance, Google has a business intelligence service. This service uses AI concepts to manage massive amounts of information and create graphs and charts to help customers make fast (and accurate) decisions.

AI and the Changing Search Landscape

In the search industry, Google uses the AI concept called deep learning. This refers to the ability of the search algorithm to adjust the results it serves based on the data collected from the behavior of people who used the same query in the past. The artificial intelligence aspect of search algorithms allow them to improve the results they serve in real time.

As an example, let's say that someone searched for the term "Superbowl News". This is a fairly common term for certain parts of the year. After completing the query, the person wasn't satisfied with the results so adjustments were made to the search term. The next query involved a different yet similar search string: "Superbowl 2018 Results". This signals the algorithm that the previously served content was unsatisfactory to the user. If thousands or millions of people do the same actions, the algorithm may choose to completely scrap the previously served results and offer other results for related queries.

Machine learning is not just used to improve the click-through rates of links in the search results page. They're also used to measure the effectiveness of rich snippets. If a user, for example, focuses his or her attention on the top parts of the page, this may mean that he or she interacted with the featured snippet. Otherwise, if the user chooses to move down in the page, this may mean that the information in the snippet is unsatisfactory. If the majority of netizens exhibit the same behavior (and yes, the search engine can detect this), the algorithm may choose to change the rich snippet result because it isn't serving the need of the users.

These are only some of the examples of how machine learning affects search services. In reality, machine learning is used in many aspects of the search algorithm. However, they are integrated so seamlessly that most people do not notice them.

Google RankBrain: the Present and the Future

Several years after their acquisition of DeepMind Technologies, Google unveiled a new machine learning algorithm that's positioned to change the web forever. Branded as RankBrain, the algorithm is classified as Artificial Narrow Intelligence (ANI). It's specifically designed to focus on automating knowledge discovery. Like other Google AIs, RankBrain has impressive deep learning capabilities. In fact, despite being new, the technology is starting to create shifts in rankings that cannot be pinpointed to specific algorithm tweaks.

For example, in the past, whenever there is a change in rankings, a specific set of rules have been applied (such as a limit in backlinks or a new requirement in relation to content quality). It does not matter whether these websites share the same niche or industry. Every website gets affected by the changes. While rankings may be "problematic" in the first few weeks or months, once SEO professionals identify those tweaks, the top ranks in SERPs start to shift back to what they once were. As we have discussed, the top ranks do not always represent the best when it comes to things that matter most to netizens.

With Google's RankBrain, these shifts in algorithms and ranks are no longer as clear. What algorithms may have been applied in one niche, might not be applied in another. It combines many core algorithms at various extents for the sake of improving user experience. For instance, RankBrain may put greater emphasis on backlink quality for websites that specifically cater to the academic crowd, while making backlinks a non-factor in those that serve as online shopping portals.

So, no matter how good SEO professionals are in finding loopholes and gaming the system, they will eventually find themselves against an AI that also reacts to their shady strategies. In the near future, gaming the system might become virtually impossible. The only way that they could win against RankBrain is by analyzing the results for each and every search. They would have to compare previous results with those after an algorithm change for the sake of identifying any tweaks made. Surely though, anything they learn from that time-consuming approach would be short lived.

While RankBrain is yet to accomplish such a feat, it improves with every bit of information it gets. It will make things increasingly difficult for anyone who intends to work around the best practices on the web. It will also make it easier for high quality websites to rank better. Most importantly, it will help refocus the entire web. Given the emphasis on staying within a website's intended niche, cross-promotional content and backlinks that barely make sense would be kept at a minimum, if not eliminated.

Would RankBrain jeopardize the SEO industry? Actually, it should help simplify things. SEO professionals who only work with white hat approaches would find optimizing sites to be a more straightforward endeavor. After all, they would no longer have to worry about loopholes that severely affect rankings. On the other hand, those who engage in black hat and grey hat SEO might run out of options. Either follow the generally accepted guidelines for improving search visibility, or continue identifying gaps in search algorithms despite the lack of lasting results.

Voice Search AI and its Positive Effects

Another reason why all SEO professionals should start playing nice is that voice-assisted search is becoming more and more accessible. Whenever you carry out a query using voice search, you will not be presented with an entire list of options such as in the case of conventional SERPs. Instead, you will only learn about the top result as the AI deems it the most appropriate response—at least in the case of Google's voice search AI. Amazon's Alexa works differently in that it will not provide answers just by searching the web.

Moving back to Google's voice search AI, note that it does not operate with mere keywords. Users typically do their search in complete sentences, as if conversing with the AI. The AI answers the query using the text found within the top search result. What happens if the top result does not have properly written content and fails to offer straightforward answers to the most basic questions (aka the five Ws)? The user might dismiss the AI's response as inaccurate or even irrelevant. So, as voice search becomes more common, website owners will have to make sure that their content is written in a clear, informative, and conversational way.

Optimizing for location will also become even more important. Many of these voice searches are done through mobile devices, particularly when travel is involved. Google's voice search AI completes queries while taking into account the user's location. Websites integrated with Google Maps will have a clear advantage. With these changes, websites with poor content, especially those made only for black hat purposes, would have a hard time staying relevant in search—reducing the harm they cause on people who are looking for information.

Knowing When Machine Learning is at Work

The only clue that we actually have that machine learning is influencing the search results is the confirmation of top Googlers themselves. Google executives have confirmed the use of machine learning concepts multiple times throughout the years.

In practice though, the effects of machine learning are so subtle that we can barely notice them. One of these effects is in the way that results are served. If you check a website's search console account, you will notice that its position is never fixed. Sometimes a given webpage is served in the top position, while in other instances it is in the second or third position. The algorithm does this because it tries to maintain variety in its results.

The selection process on which content to serve in first, second, and third positions all depends on the algorithm and the data that it is fed. Google's network of services collects data on the behavior of thousands or millions of people that use a particular query. It then uses this data to make the real-time decisions on which webpage will serve the needs of the current users. In short, the search algorithm learns from the behavior of the people who used a particular query in the past.

This principle also works in the way that Google serves ads. It's important to remember that Google is focused on long-term profit. With this in mind, we could understand why it would choose to serve ads that prioritize user experience rather than profit. This is the reason why Google and other search engines try to avoid ads that may cause financial harm to the user. For example, Google bans content and ads that relate to gambling. In recent years, they have also cracked down on ads related to services that infringe intellectual property and high risk financial assets.

The Shortcomings of AI Technology

Truth be told, deep learning is an effective tool in improving search technology. However, it is not yet perfect and many pundits are arguing against its wide use in search networks.

Aside from the standard search algorithm, Google is also using AI in processing information that was impossible to process in the past. In particular, Google has been developing its AI technology for processing images and videos. With the help of deep learning, Google has significantly improved image suggestions. AI technology has allowed the search giant to let go of its reliance on the alt-tag when it comes to ranking images.

AI technology, no matter how impressive it has become, is still in its early days. While it's easy to think that we are living in the future, the truth is that AI isn't successful yet even in the simplest of tasks. This has been proven quite recently when YouTube failed to detect that one of the videos of a well-known YouTube artist had a dead body in it.

The video spread like wildfire in the platform and was shared countless times before it was ultimately taken down because of the massive backlash. As expected, the company blamed the artist for this video and washed their hands of the whole thing by saying that their platform is maintained by algorithms and sometimes these algorithms make mistakes.

Clearly, this is a sign that the technology is not yet close to achieving what it's supposed to achieve. Even one of the biggest tech conglomerates in the world has failed in keeping its own network safe. AI has failed in keeping a network that's full kids, kid friendly.

Future of Artificial Intelligence and Marketing

We are now seeing the most advanced machine learning technologies being launched. So far though, only conglomerates are using AI for marketing. However, it won't be long before it will be commercially available (or in other words, financially accessible) to all. The idea of machines replacing humans is becoming too real. One of the areas where it will be first introduced is online marketing. Machine learning has the advantage of reacting to generated data in real time.

In the world of investments, for example, we are already seeing AI being used to replace traders in making buying and selling decisions. We will see a similar application of the technology in the marketing industry. Right now, marketing companies are still relying on their employees when it comes to making decisions. While online marketing is the most data-driven form of marketing, it is still more art than a science. The creative part of marketing still lies in the hands of people. And yet, as often pointed out by technology purists, people are prone to making mistakes based on personal biases.

As of the writing of this book, there are already AI companies working on changing all this. They're developing bots that are designed to identify the visual elements of ads and their relative success. This has been the trend of AI technology. First comes data gathering. And if an AI is better equipped with the algorithm to judge visual elements of a digital environment, the next step will be creation.

It's expected that AIs will be producing marketing materials in the future. In addition, they will also carry out marketing strategies, gather data, and automate the entire process of data analysis. An artist, for example, could be guided by an AI based on the data of the most common and most successful marketing art on the internet. This not only applies to text and web ads either. It could also be applied to GIFs and videos.

The applications of artificial intelligence technologies are endless and Google is in the forefront of all of this. Right now, the search giant is already experimenting on ways in letting AI decide on what ads to serve people. They're also working on predicting user behavior, thereby preventing ad-click frauds. In Google's other applications, the company is also using AI to try to stop spam emails from reaching the inboxes of Gmail accounts. In a similar way, it's also using AI to find spam websites used to boost links profiles.

Because AI technologies are completely digital and our robotics technology is still at its infancy, it is only logical that the first implementation of AI technologies will start on the web. As the technology becomes more common, we could expect some consumer-level marketing services to offer AI-based technologies in the future. In the search marketing industry, for example, this could be applied in hastening the processes of keyword research, content curation, and link building. It could also be applied in the monetization process, with the goal of improving ad relevance, achieving proper redirects based on user demographics, and doing online business intelligence.

As of the moment, the processes we enumerated above all use some form of big data analysis to make marketing decisions. With AI, however, the decisions will be narrowed down by the technology itself.

Danger of Too Much Artificial Intelligence

The introduction of new technology always has some negative effects. In the case of AI, people are starting to fear for their jobs. Even Alphabet Inc. CEO Larry Page, said that the danger of people losing jobs to AI based technologies is real.

Here's an example that illustrates the technology's potential: AI could be taught to write programming languages for specific purposes based on the best practices that are already used today. If successful, coding may become more accessible to even non-engineers, thereby making programming skills obsolete.

Companies are also experimenting on the use of AI as a replacement for customer service representatives. In the recent years, AI technologies with the ability to speak have been introduced to the public. It will not be long before these speaking robots will be introduced to the market to provide customer support for big industries like telecommunication, banking and finance, and computer hardware and software. Google may even be one of the first companies to offer this service.

While it is possible for this innovation to happen within the next couple of years, we could expect the early iterations of this technology to have a less than satisfactory performance. However, because AI has the ability to learn, it can possibly learn from each interaction and improve whatever service is being provided.

The danger of this, of course, is when AIs become much smarter than humans. While theories like this seem like something that you would hear a crazy person say, we should not rule it out as science fiction. While we are discussing the subject of AI, let's also explore the areas where it can be used against consumers.

Companies generally hate the customer service sections of their operations because these groups of employees are non-income generating. Because of this, most companies try to monetize these parts of the company to justify their existence. We should not expect this trend to stop even though AI technologies have completely replaced their human counterparts.

Imagine an AI who knows how to sell. Now, imagine that AI learning with each sales interaction. This is just one of the possible outcomes of this new technology. And it is rest assured that companies are looking for other ways to make this new technology more profitable.

Chapter 9 - The Dark World of Internet Marketing

While search engines are already some of our most advanced forms of technology, they still have limitations. These limitations can sometimes be used as exploits by online marketers who just want to make a quick buck off of unsuspecting online users. Some of their techniques are used to manipulate rankings, while others are used to make you click and buy from their websites.

Cheating with Content

Publishing Click-bait Content

Click-baiting is a recently developed technique and is more commonly used in social media. However, now that Facebook has cut down the reach of business pages in their users' newsfeeds, it's become harder for most marketers to organically reach their followers. As a result, they rely on their click-bait techniques in other areas of the internet, such as in the search engines.

The idea is to create a headline and meta description that will catch the attention of the user. The marketers focus on these two features because they are the ones that show up in the page preview. Simply put, when a webpage appears in the search results page, users will only see these elements.

While making the SEO title and meta description engaging isn't a crime, fooling people into clicking on them is almost one. The malpractice happens when the marketer uses misleading or incomplete titles and descriptions to entice users to click. They usually create outrageous claims in these elements to stir the curiosity of netizens. Sometimes they would take it one step further than just stretching the truth.

This is one of the reasons why every now and again, you see fake news about the death of a popular celebrity. Marketers keep using them because the headline makes people click on their links.

In case you are wondering what click-bait actually looks like, well, here are a few examples (these are spun or rewritten in so many ways, but the general idea remains the same):

- You'll never guess why...
- Our discovery will surprise you
- The biggest companies hate this guy
- Here's why we chose the second best
- These facts will forever change your life
- This unbelievable trick will save your job
- This article will definitely blow your mind
- You'll be shocked with what happens next

There's a reason why Facebook and Twitter penalize pages and accounts that make use of this technique. However, the method is still rampantly used in search platforms, including Google. If you are among those who endlessly wonder why these "headlines" still work despite the fact that people are already so aware of their existence, you simply have to consider how the mind works. Whenever it detects any obvious gap in knowledge, it develops a strong urge to fill that gap.

Spinning Articles

We have already discussed the key concept of article spinning in previous chapters. Simply put, it is the process of rewriting existing articles to come up with "fresh" content. Why do marketers do this when they can copy entire articles and put them on their websites? Well, they can't—or rather, they would not want to risk getting penalized. Duplicate content spam could result to a drop in ranking, and may even get a website deindexed.

Spinning is typically done in two ways. The first one involves the use of applications to automate the rewriting process. These can easily be found online and many can be used free of charge (such as SmallSEOTools' Article Rewriter). The second method is to hire a professional article spinner, usually through freelancing hubs like Upwork.

As you can surely imagine, there's a noticeable gap in the quality between these two options. Even premium or subscription-based automated spinners won't be able to churn out articles on par with those written by an actual person (assuming that he or she is at least competent). It would even be safe to say that relying on skilled writers is a surefire way of avoiding Google's patented duplicate content detection system. Other search engines will also have difficulty detecting carefully rewritten or spun content.

Investing in article spinning services will impact a marketer's budget (spending anywhere from 10 to 50 USD per hour if he or she wishes to work with an experienced writer). However, coming up with articles that are entirely original and provide the newest information will obviously cost a lot more.

Engaging in Bait and Switch

Have you ever clicked on a link that led you to a completely unrelated page under the same site? This is how bait and switch typically works on SERPs. Groupon, for example, faced a lawsuit back in 2011 upon engaging in such a misleading marketing technique. The company had these ads for play areas in Google, but people who clicked on them landed in entirely different product pages, such as those for photo-to-canvas print services.

They were also associated with false discount claims, particularly for their travel packages. People would be tempted by their links that claimed to offer discounts of at least 50 percent. However, upon clicking on the links, none of the discounts were really offered (despite all other details being correct).

Expedia is a more recent example of known companies that tried to do bait and switch. Expedia is a website that specifically caters to those looking to book tickets and hotel rooms, though they do offer other travel-related services. Their use of this shady strategy was a bit more creative compared to Groupon's. The travel booking company worked hard to get the top ranks in search for Buckeye Tree Lodge. Note that this inn isn't part of Expedia's booking program.

When people clicked on the seemingly official links, they were redirected to either blank pages or websites that showcase Expedia's partner properties. While some would attempt to find Buckeye Tree Lodge's actual website, there are individuals who would surely end up thinking that the inn's online booking system just isn't available—and so, they would choose to book with another place.

Although bait and switch can help increase both traffic and sales, it is more harmful in the long run. As we have discussed in a previous chapter, bounce rate could very well be among the hidden factors that drive search visibility. And it is likely for a person to just return to the SERP upon being tricked into accessing an unrelated or inaccurate page. Customer trust also takes a hit with this approach.

Scraping Pages and Websites

Like bait and switch, this is not just risky in terms of getting penalized by search engines. There is the possibility of getting sued for scraping web content since it goes against copyright laws. Scraping is usually done through specialized software, but it can also be manually accomplished by copying and reposting content. Although Google penalizes websites hosting scraped content, it still isn't as effective as it should be in that regard.

Given that suing scrapers is not always an option (especially for bloggers, given their limited resources), setting up defenses against scraping is the best way to go. There are programs that identify bots and afterwards block their IPs. Likewise, there are ways to block bot activity through code (typically in JavaScript). Website owners who are a bit on the feisty side tend to leave links on the pages containing duplicate content. This allows them to get a bit of link juice.

For companies worried about having their content stolen, there are software solutions that search the web for possible duplicates. The problem with these, however, is that using them could be against Google's policies on automated queries.

Excessive Optimization

Adding Invisible Text

This is among the earliest "cheats" in SEO and internet marketing. During the early 2000s, having the right keywords and using them as many times as possible is a surefire way of improving search visibility. The problem with this approach is that visitors won't appreciate a webpage loaded with keywords, especially since it has a significant effect on content quality.

Of course, someone came up with the idea of hiding text by matching their color with that of the page's. Eventually other similar techniques were developed, such as moving the text outside the visible area instead of merely changing its color. There are also website owners who added links through these means.

While adding invisible text worked for quite some time, they no longer offer any benefit these days. In fact, those who make the mistake of doing this end up getting their sites penalized.

Just to be perfectly clear though, this black hat technique is not the same as adding alt text for images. Alt text are important in letting search engines know about the images that appear on a page. This is extremely important in ensuring accessibility, as well as in improving functionality and compatibility with both voice search and voice recognition.

Using Unrelated Keywords

Though sometimes used for bait and switch, using unrelated keywords can be done purely for ranking purposes. SEO professionals who guarantee first-page placement often rely on this method to make things easier for them. While seeing a website among the top results may seem impressive, it should be for a suitable keyword. Not having the right keywords actually prevents a website from generating valuable traffic.

Most people would simply go back to the SERP upon seeing irrelevant content. Some would not even click on the link upon noticing that the domain or address itself is barely related to what they are looking for. As we have discussed in a previous chapter, having a high bounce rate could negatively affect search visibility. And so, even among black hat techniques, using unrelated keywords is arguably the least useful yet most harmful.

Getting Ahead with Links

Exchanging or Buying Links

Prior to Panda and Penguin, exchanging or buying links worked like a charm. Website owners would receive messages containing a simple request—that a provided link would be posted on their site in exchange of having one of their links posted on the sender's website. Likewise, there are those who outright offer link placement in exchange for cash. After Google's massive algorithm updates, countless sites that benefited from this trick suffered massive losses in traffic. Some were even completely removed from SERPs.

Why did this happen? The answer lies in the fact that many of these link swaps or sales involved entirely unrelated websites. Site owners that got hundreds of inbound links in a short span of time, even when relevance was considered, also faced penalties. Keep in mind, however, that exchanging links is not prohibited by Google and other search engines. It's the attempt to artificially improve PageRank in the fastest, simplest way possible that is considered a violation.

Anything done purely for cross-linking purposes can potentially harm a website's search visibility. And so, many SEO professionals who continue this practice try to do things discreetly, being mindful of the pace at which they are getting (and giving) links. Until search engines can develop an automated way of accurately detecting link sales and exchanges, this black hat strategy will continue to affect search experience.

Filling Press Releases with Links

Press releases posted on other websites may seem harmless enough, but they can be used as carriers of links. Although one or two per press release article is perfectly fine, there are those that feature excessively optimized anchor text. This means that almost every relevant keyword in the post is linked to a particular page or site. Unnatural links and link placement are in violation of Google's quality guidelines.

Here's an example of excessively optimized anchor text use (assume that all underlined words or phrases are linked):

Although mobile phones have become the most used communication device, pagers are still the smarter choice given their size. Combined with the latest technologies, pagers now offer everything a mobile can. Text messages and calls without the bulk is here at last!

"Our aim is to put an end to the dominance of mobile phones throughout the world. By offering pagers that anyone can afford, use, and trust, we're confident that people will choose us," said Eric Goode (Pagerrific Inc. CEO).

SERPs and their Loopholes

Sending Automated Queries to Search Engines

Back in the early 2000s, web marketers and site owners relied on tools that automatically sent queries to Google and other search engines for the sake of tracking rankings and other relevant search data. Initially, at least in the case of Google, this was allowed through the use of the SOAP API Search Key. Once this was discontinued, however, people relied on tools that carried out the same function, albeit through other means—by screen-scraping the SERPs.

Screen-scraping is an automated process in which a program captures display data (in this case, the SERP) and turns that data into actual information, such as those related to rankings for specific queries. This is against Google's Terms of Service, but people did it anyway. The search giant solved this concern by improving their automated query detection system, blocking any IP that's likely being used for such purpose. Even though these automated query programs were eventually upgraded to simulate the movements of a real person to avoid detection, they were no match for Google's ever-improving system.

Now, you are probably wondering why the search engine company is being so strict when it comes to sending automated queries. For one, the queries themselves can (and do) affect the number of searches for specific keywords or search strings. Another reason could be related to the unnecessary burden that automated queries put on the search engine's servers, possibly affecting the speed at which search results are provided to all users.

Using Rich Snippet to Beat Superior Content

The rich snippet feature is becoming more common in Google search. With each day, more and more queries get their own version of the rich snippet. SEO professionals know that these features are effective in grabbing people's attention. For some queries, it's even more effective to be the source of the rich snippet than to rank first in the search results page. The goal is to be the first in the ranking and also be the one featured as the source of the rich snippet.

Some website owners, however, aren't knowledgeable enough on how to have their pages featured as a search result snippet. As to be expected, they're usually beaten by webmasters who specialize in using these snippets to grab traffic. The problem happens when the content of the rich snippet's source is not superior to that of the top page.

This happens because of the difference in the criteria of being the source of the rich snippet and being on top of the Google search results page. Usually, the algorithm ranking the pages are more critical of content value and user experience. On the other hand, for your webpage content to be featured as a rich snippet, you only need to make sure that you've coded the page properly.

Dishonest Site Development

Engaging in Typosquatting

Typosquatting is another term for fake URL. It takes advantage of the common mistakes in keying in the URL of a site. For example, in the mid 1990s, People for the Ethical Treatment of Animals (PETA) had their website under the com top-level domain. Now, someone realized that PETA.org was still available and grabbed it to make an online hub for a different kind of PETA: People Eating Tasty Animals.

While that person was nice enough to add a link to PETA.com for netizens who are into vegetarianism and eco-activism, he still ended up being sued by the animal rights organization. The organization won and were handed the PETA.org domain, but the one behind People Eating Tasty Animals was not given any fine whatsoever. The judge deemed that there is no grounds for infringement or any other offense.

Obviously, typosquatting can be used in a more malicious way. For example, the fake URL could contain a scraped copy of the correct website, with all the download links replaced with malware-containing software or files. Alternatively, the copycat can be loaded with ads for quick monetary gain. Unwary visitors may even think that the companies being featured in such ads are recommended by those running the original website.

In the US, there is a law specifically passed to curb typosquatting—the Anticybersquatting Consumer Protection Act (ACPA). Legally though, the acquisition of a misspelled domain can only be considered typosquatting if there is an attempt to catch and exploit traffic for monetary gain. Despite having occurred before the law was passed, the PETA situation does shed light on what is considered malicious when it comes to acquiring misspelled website addresses.

Changing Homepage and Search Settings

Sites can be developed in such a way that they automatically make tweaks to key browser settings (such as the homepage and the default search engine) and prevent such changes from being undone. This sends traffic to these sites and search portals, which in turn generates cash for the ones behind this underhanded tactic. Depending on how the tweaks were made, it might be necessary to do a browser refresh (reverting the browser to its factory state).

It's important to know, however, that not all websites that affect your browser's settings without confirmation were actually made to accomplish such a thing. For example, hackers can inject malicious code into a WordPress website's header. If Google suspects that a website has been injected with potentially dangerous code, they might add a "This site may be hacked" note under the URL if it appears in their SERPs.

Fortunately for honest site owners and SEO professionals, Google allows them to file reconsideration requests through the Google Search Console. As to be expected though, the search giant won't be providing much help in ridding a website of malicious code. Still, there are web security companies (such as VirusTotal and Norton) that offer free tools for quick script and redirect detection. Once identified, malicious code can be easily removed.

Taking over the first page

Taking over then first page is a strategy that tries to get all rank positions on the first page. They create fake competitors with different names and website layouts, fake blogs, fake reference sites, fake review sites, fake fans and run SEO strategies in all of those links together so they can remove all real competitors from the first page.

Making Doorway Sites or Pages

Though arguably not as bad as the previous two, making doorway sites or pages still has a negative effect on user experience. These sites or pages are made specifically to achieve the highest possible placement in SERPs, sometimes taking multiple spots on the same page. Despite having distinct URLs, doorways direct the user to the same page. What's worse is that some doorway sites or pages funnel users through intermediate pages to maximize traffic and time on site.

Aggressive Attacks

Tapping into Negative SEO

As we have discussed in a previous chapter, Google's strictness when it comes to quality and relevance can be used to carry out attacks. Negative SEO, following the concept of the backlink paradox, is done by associating unnatural and suspicious backlinks to the target site. This is also accomplished in the fastest possible way to increase the chances of Google flagging the site for multiple guideline violations.

What makes this attack so dangerous, however, is the sheer difficulty of detecting it early. Moreover, finding the culprit is nearly impossible. Even well-known SEO companies can have their search visibility severely affected by negative SEO. In 2014, Jellyfish UK, a successful digital marketing agency, saw a massive drop in their site's search performance. After investigating the issue, they identified more than a thousand unnatural backlinks mostly in the form of comment spam.

Recovering from the attack required Jellyfish UK to get in touch with site administrators to ask for link removal. For instances in which that approach is not applicable, the digital marketing agency had to rely on Google Disavow. This stops Google from considering certain links (or sources of links) in evaluating a site. Used improperly, Google Disavow can harm a site's search performance—and so, even the search giant recommends that it should only be used in cases where there is no other option of taking down bad links.

Jellyfish UK survived the ordeal largely due to their familiarity with the intricacies of SEO. If this happens to a popular website that is being run by someone not as well versed, timely detection and recovery would be highly unlikely. With black hats becoming more creative and aggressive in their approach, honest SEO professionals and site owners can only hope that search engines are coming up with ways of countering negative SEO.

Spamming Social Networking Platforms

With the reach of social networking platforms, it's not at all surprising that black hats are starting to move towards them. Comments containing malicious links are being spread throughout social media, and those who end up clicking on these links become unwilling participants in driving traffic (and in turn, cash) towards shady sites.

For example, you've been browsing your Facebook feed and you came across an interesting comment that points to a link. Despite the risk involved, you chose to click on the link. In a matter of seconds, your device was infected with malware and you're getting bombarded with popups. As you try to close each of them, new ones start to appear. It becomes a never ending battle until you give up and either live with the problem or choose to clear your device.

Most malware can be removed by a memory wipe, especially in the case of Android. However, some are specifically designed to survive the function, reinstalling themselves through a compromised sync function or setting themselves as a system app. There are even rare reports of malware infecting the BIOS of a device, making removal nearly impossible even for experts.

Google is aware of this, but their options in blocking links from social media is currently limited despite the SEO-driven end goal of link spams. They do, however, show warnings about unsafe sites under Chrome. Other browsers have similar functionality as well.

Consumer Manipulation

Using A/B n Testing To Get Attention

Have you ever wondered how many companies online make design decisions? They do this through a process called A/B n Testing. To carry out this strategy, they create multiple versions of a webpage and use a software to randomly serve them to users going to one URL. Some websites, for example, would have five or more URL versions to begin with. With each person that arrives at the page, the online marketers gather data that are related to their goal for the website.

After presenting the different webpages and gathering enough data, the marketers analyze the numbers to identify the parts of the website that increase the likelihood that users will do their desired action. This action is usually connected with the needs of the business. A startup, for example, may focus on making people sign up for a service or an email subscription. An ecommerce website, on the other hand, may use this technique to increase sales numbers. While A/B n testing is usually a harmless method, some companies use it for more nefarious purposes. In particular, they could be used to funnel users into giving financial information. A children's games website, for instance, could use the technique to direct the attention of children from games towards buying toys.

Some websites also use A/B n testing to encourage upgrades on accounts. It's common, for example, for teens to tweak their own mobile phone plans without the consent of the parents. They can do this by accessing their account through the telecom company's website. Once they are logged in, they become victims to the effects of A/B n testing methods. The design features of the website are meant to get the attention of the users and to make them do specific actions. Most of the time, the parents will only know about their children's actions when they get a huge bill on the following month.

Customer Service as a Way to Sell

Big companies today also know that netizens usually use search engines to look for customer service options. While some customer service methods can only be done through email, many companies are now offering customer service on their website through chat. While this new feature may seem like a step in the right direction, its actually still a profitmaking move for these giant companies. For each dollar that they spend on these customer service options, they expect a few more in return through additional sales, service upgrades, and referrals.

The downside is that, Google and other search engine firms seem to favor these websites because they naturally climb high for branded search terms. If you search for the search term "AT&T customer chat support" for example, you will be led to the website of the telecom giant. Once you are connected with a representative, they will pounce on every opportunity they get to sell you things. Some of them are also incentivized to do this through additional commission.

Creating Fake Authority Figures

As Google's algorithm increased its preference towards authority websites, it became apparent to many online marketers that they can no longer sell through websites with thin content. The ones who survived did so by creating so-called authority websites.

In these websites, they create a lot of long-form content for a specific niche topic and create the illusion that there are real people behind the website. In reality, the photos of the people they feature on their websites are merely stock images. And the long-form content that they present to their users are just information curated from different websites and rewritten to pass off as original content.

These marketers know that people are more likely to trust their website content if they have experts posted as the authors of their articles. However, many of them cannot afford to work with real experts because that would mean they will be dividing their income with another person. An easier alternative is to create a fake person from generic-looking stock photos—and this is what most of them do. In reality, it's the online marketer or one of his or her virtual assistants who write the content.

Fake authority figures like these are all too common on the internet today. Google and other search engines haven't found a way yet to check the credibility of each author in the search results they present. This may cause big problems when the user trusts the information that isn't fact-checked by the website's owner.

Using Gamification to Drive Actions

Gamification is another buzzword in the online marketing industry that has a big impact in the way people interact with websites and apps. While this strategy is mostly used on mobile apps, many website owners also use this technique to increase engagement and user retention. Most importantly, it's extremely effective in increasing sales numbers.

The practices used in gamification stem from early psychology theories like classical conditioning theory and behaviorism. However, the most widely used is BF Skinner's operant conditioning theory. The idea is that a person, in this case the website developer, can manipulate the behaviors of people by controlling the reward-and-punishment mechanism of a system. So, in this context, the website is the system and its features can be used as the delivery system for the reward or punishment.

One common feature among gamified sites is the rewarding and deducting of points that can be used as currency in the controlled system. One example of this is when a website owner rewards the user with points when he or she comes back to the website for a specific number of days in a month. Likewise, the website owner could reward points for users who participate in the forum of the website. The rank of the users could also increase when he or she accumulates enough number of points.

This concept could then be used to reward the behaviors of the user that generate profit for the website. For example, in forums and Q&A websites, you will often find a point reward system wherein members are rewarded when they provide useful content that others up-vote. When properly implemented, the system can encourage people do profitable actions like creating user-generated content for the website. It could also be utilized to make people promote the website. Including a social aspect to the gamification system can also increase the frequency of a certain behavior. Social rewards (like virtual achievement trophies) can be handed out to people who participate in the website. You will notice these types of systems in membership-based websites.

Gamification is effective not only as an engagement tool but also as a supporting feature for SEO. A properly gamified website will have increased activity, thereby getting better user engagement signals as well. It increases time on page as well as the number of direct traffic going to the website. A high amount of direct traffic tells Google that the website has a lot of regular visitors. It suggests that the website is a great brand or an authority in their niche.

Gamification works because it uses our psychological biases to increase the frequency of certain behaviors. The reward-or-punishment system works in creating positive or negative feelings. When the user receives a reward immediately after a specific behavior, he or she feels good because of it. The positive feeling is similar to that of a preschooler who received a star from the teacher for doing school work. The star in itself has no intrinsic value. However, the idea of being rewarded makes the person feel good. If the reward is publicly announced like in the trophy achievement system in web and mobile apps, it also acts as a social reward. A person with more achievements, for example, will likely feel like an authority in the online community. In the process, that person will continue to look for more achievements.

Punishments and negative reinforcement also work as effectively in deterring certain behaviors. Using gamification, a website owner can punish people who create poor content. People who do not participate could also be punished. The punishment could be in the form of suspension or a warning. In a sales website, for instance, a person with the least amount of sales could be punished through public shaming. His or her photo could be posted in the website for the others to see. This sort of social punishment will create a negative emotion in the users.

While punishments can sometimes work in an autocratic community, it often does not work in a free market system where people can just leave your website if they feel bad. In these types of systems, negative reinforcement is more likely to be used by website owners.

Negative reinforcement is the removal of an advantage if the person does not perform the desired behavior. Let's say that every member of a website starts out with one hundred percent access to all services. However, when they sign up, they are told that some of the perks of being a new member will be removed if the member does not refer a new person to the website within a year. This is an example of a negative reinforcement. In this case, you are not adding suffering or making things difficult for the users. Instead, you are removing a positive feeling that the user once felt.

Negative reinforcement could also be applied through the removal of points or achievements. This will remove any positive social feeling that the user once had. The idea is that they will try to work and regain whatever it is that they lost because of negative reinforcement.

Gamification often leads to Addiction

Now that you know how gamification works, you will start to notice how often it is used in our digital world. It's widely used in social media apps but they are also becoming more prevalent among websites with membership features.

While gamification can also be used for good, its effects are mostly negative. This is especially true when the gamification system encourages addiction. Most gamification features in websites are used to increase participation and frequency of visit. People are usually rewarded to reinforce behavior like going back to the website on a daily basis, adding one post each day, or sharing unique content. By reinforcing these types of behaviors, the webmaster aims to make users build a habit of returning to the website. The user will willingly return to the website and do the tasks that are rewarded by the system because they wish to increase the number of achievements they have.

In some cases though, people become so hooked in these gamification features that they will miss important real-life events to be with their online community. The gamification system creates a false sense of achievement and authority among members who have the highest rank or those with the most achievements.

Data Scraping and Demographic Targeting

Not all people fall for the manipulative practices we've discussed so far in this chapter. People with a well-developed metacognitive skill are likely to detect manipulative practices before they happen, preventing themselves from falling for them. Online marketers know this and are smart enough not to target these people. Instead, they target those who are more likely to fall for their engagement traps.

Online marketers use psychological theories and online statistics to identify those more likely to fall for these manipulation techniques. For example, it has been proven that people in the 21-25 age group are more likely to fall for these techniques than those in older age groups. Likewise, the stats show that those younger than 21 fall for these tricks as well. However, because it's usually illegal in most states to target minors with marketing materials, online marketers generally avoid them.

People in the 21-25 age group are the better target because aside from being more susceptible to digital manipulation, they also have more spending power than those younger than them. Most importantly, they're legally allowed to enter financial commitments without the need for a guardian.

While age is a common targeting information for most online marketers, there are other demographic data that can help online marketers in increasing their manipulation success rate. Certain companies, for instance, reinforce activities that are more likely to be done by a specific gender. Others also try to target people interested in specific types of content. People who constantly use search terms related to religion and politics are likely to become emotional about these topics. All in all, online marketers usually use between ten and a hundred demographic-defining data to help them in their campaigns.

You may be wondering how these online marketers actually use the data to get the attention of their target online users. While each online marketer has a different strategy, using paid methods is as common strategy. In search, Google AdWords is one of the most commonly used tools for specific targeting for online marketing campaigns.

AdWords is unique from other ad platforms because it's specifically made for Google search. The search terms used by the user are usually the primary targeting data for the campaign. Google AdWords also has targeting features for demographic data like gender, age, parental status, and household income. Household income data is available only for video campaigns and is currently only available for AdWords advertisers in the US, Japan, New Zealand, and Australia.

While Google's targeting features are not as specific as that of social networks like Facebook, their tools can generate better revenue for marketers because of the ability to use search terms. Targeting specific search terms have proven to be effective for most advertisers selling specific products or services.

In the beginning, online marketers used organic and paid campaigns with general targeting to get traction for their websites. Once they've gained enough online users, they then try to mine demographic data from them. They could do this in a variety of ways. A membership website, for instance, could use a membership form to collect data from users. Some of them could utilize automatic online registration with the help of common membership websites like Google and Facebook. This hassle-free registration process increases the number of signups in a website.

Online marketers collect loads of user data through this approach. At the very least, they will be able to see the email addresses of those who signed up. If a person used a service like Facebook to automatically sign up with the website, the marketers will also have access to a lot more types of data. In the registration process, the website will declare what types of data they will need from your Facebook account. Most people just register in these websites without really reviewing the kinds of data that will be accessed. In some cases, a website or app will access only basic user information. However, some websites and apps are specifically designed for data gathering.

A website, for example, could request access to your friends list, your contact number, and even your location.

They could then use the data collected from you and all the other members of the website to create a general profile of their target users. Using different ads platforms like Google AdWords, they will then use these mined data as the basis for ads targeting. This method allows online marketers to target specific types of people. In fact, if you collect the demographic data of your family members, you can even target them using these online ads platforms. That's how effective modern targeting tools are.

Manipulating People through Landing Pages

After luring you into their website, online marketers use a variety of methods to get you to do the tasks they want. One of the most commonly used tool for this is the landing page. A landing page is the term used by online marketers for the page where you are redirected to after clicking on an ad. A landing page could just be a regular webpage on a website. It may have all the features common to all the pages in the said website. However, marketers who want short-term success from their efforts often optimize their landing pages to increase conversion.

They do this by stripping that single page of any link that may allow the user to check another page. The only link on the page is usually the one that leads to conversion. Most often, this is a link to the checkout cart. This prevents users from getting distracted by extra features that are commonly added to webpages. The only options for users are to either go on with the purchase or to close the tab or press back.

Another technique they use is through adjusting content specifically for the landing page. Most landing pages do not look like your usual product page. Instead, they are usually designed to have content related to the sale. This is called the sales copy. Online marketers use different copywriting techniques to increase their success. One of the most common of these copywriting techniques is to appeal to the user's emotions. A website selling security cameras, for example, may start their copy with a line like this:

"Are your kids safe at night?"

A question like this would make the heart of any parent skip a beat. And that's exactly what online marketers want. They usually use the words in their copy to make people feel fear, because fear is one of the best emotions to tap into when trying to sell something. In fact, when online marketers are trying to invoke emotion with their copies, they're more likely to use negative emotions. Positive emotions have been statistically proven to be less motivating in sales. On the other hand, negative emotions are more likely to make a person feel uncomfortable, which in turn leads to better chances of conversion.

Online marketers aim to make you buy or subscribe to a service by presenting their product as the solution to the problem that's causing you to have that emotion. They make it seem that buying their product will help you deal with the problem when in reality, you never would have thought about that problem if they didn't bring it up. The words they use will make it seem like they are your friends and that they are there to help you. By now though, we know that they're only there because they want to sell you something.

Targeting Children and the Elderly

Most of you reading this may be thinking that this will never happen to you. In fact, many of the people who hear of these black hat methods think that this is a victimless crime.

While you may not be the victim of these malpractices, it does not mean that other people do not fall for them. In fact, the victims of these crimes are usually those members of our society who are not skilled enough in spotting scams and poor advice. In general, this usually involves the young and the elderly. The former are yet to learn that there are parts of the society who are willing to fool them to make money. The latter, on the other hand, are not skilled enough to know about the different tricks used these days. Because of these reasons, they are the most likely victims of these crimes.

While Google's search and ads technologies are the most advanced in the world, they do not protect these people from the ploys of online marketing. Online marketers treat people and their behaviors like numbers on a screen. They don't care if they are selling to a minor or an elderly. They only focus on their earnings.

In the case of minors, there's also no point in giving the responsibility to parents. Most children today (particularly those older than 10 years old) are more tech savvy that their own parents. Many kids know how to bypass the parental control features of devices. The older they get, the easier it becomes for them to hack these systems and start using apps and accessing prohibited websites.

Google and other search engines must act as a gatekeeper for these types of users. While there are some features that may protect kids and the elderly, the ones that we have now are not enough. These companies must set it as one of their priorities to uphold their corporate responsibilities to the consumers they serve.

Final Words

The entire search industry, just like the rest of the businesses in the world, are not perfect. They make mistakes and they continue to improve with each passing day. However, there are those who would argue that search engine firms are not taking enough responsibility in keeping the internet a safe place. Besides, as some would say, there's a chance that they're not even trying to take responsibility—maybe they're only in this for the money.

With all the possibilities and what-ifs, we really shouldn't let them safeguard our every information. If you're starting to trust search engine companies a bit too much, just remember that Facebook essentially gave all sorts of excuses when Mark Zuckerberg was interviewed in Congress for when the Russians used their ad network. Also, as we've discussed, reliance on AI when the technology is extremely young can cause many more issues in the near future. If our country has trouble detecting how our tech giants are being used by outside forces, so will other countries with far less technological capabilities.

Besides, even if these search engine firms are really doing their best in keeping the web a secure place for all, shady online marketers and the black hat crowd have always managed to stay one step ahead. With every change made to the guidelines, policies, and even algorithms involving search engines, these people never fail to find loopholes. Despite how far things have come, the online world is still filled with poor and potentially dangerous content. Countless people get tricked on a daily basis, and money is no longer the only thing at stake—personal information has become a precious commodity in today's interconnected world.

So, whether you believe that these search engine companies are to blame or they are doing their best in maintaining safety and quality throughout the web, keep in mind that there are dark secrets at play. It would only be wise to stay alert whenever you're exploring online. Don't believe every content you find, and think twice before clicking on the next link you see—even if it has the top spot in the SERP.

If you liked this book please give it a positive review on Amazon. If you feel like there is room for improvements, or if you have any doubts, please get in contact with the author at fernandoybus.com and leave a message. The author will be very happy to help you.

Thank you again for reading this book!

www.ingramcontent.com/pod-product-compliance
Lightning Source LLC
Chambersburg PA
CBHW020546220526
45463CB00006B/2208